collector's guide
CIGARETTE *Lighters*

Book II

James Flanagan

COLLECTOR BOOKS
A Division of Schroeder Publishing Co., Inc.

Searching For A Publisher?

We are always looking for knowledgable people considered to be experts within their fields. If you feel that there is a real need for a book on your collectible subject and have a large comprehensive collection, contact Collector Books.

Book design by: Karen Long
Cover design by: Beth Summers

Additional copies of this book may be ordered from:

COLLECTOR BOOKS
P.O. Box 3009
Paducah, KY 42002–3009

@$17.95. Add $2.00 for postage and handling.

Copyright: James Flanagan, 1996

Printed by IMAGE GRAPHICS, INC., Paducah, Kentucky

— DEDICATION —

Once again I dedicate this book to my best friend and loving wife, Patricia. Her help and encouragement kept me going to get this book done.

— ON THE COVER —

Top (l to r): Brass and ceramic table lighter made by Evans. $30.00 – 50.00. Marble base with gold-plated lighter made by Alfred Dunhill. $250.00 – 300.00. Chromium and blue marble-like plastic made in Japan (unique lighter mechanism). $20.00 – 30.00. **Bottom (l to r):** Reproduction of Ronson's "Banjo" pocket lighter, brass finish with a floral design. $40.00 – 60.00. Chromium and ceramic elephant table lighter made in Occupied Japan. $60.00 – 90.00. Chromium pocket lighter with decals on front and back made in Japan. $10.00 – 15.00.

— ACKNOWLEDGMENTS —

— *To my wonderful children, Teresa, Lisa, and Jimmy for their support and for spending hours at shows and antique stores looking for lighters for my collection.*

— *Once again to Judy Reilly for the wonderful job she did photographing the lighters and accessories.*

— *To my father Melvin Flanagan for always being on the look out, no matter where he is, for lighters to add to my collection.*

— *To my mother Marie Bowser for lighters she has given to me.*

— *To all the friends I have made at antique shows, shops, and through the lighter clubs.*

— *Thanks very much to all of you.*

— CONTENTS —

— INTRODUCTION —

Welcome to the second volume of *Collector's Guide to Cigarette Lighters.* This volume contains more common everyday lighters as well as more very rare and unusual ones.

While there might be some similarity, all the lighters are different than the ones in the first publication.

You will find lighters that were made with just ladies in mind. Unique lighter/cases that also had make-up compartments. This type of lighter became popular when women started smoking in public. There are also men's lighter/cases. They were a popular item too, especially ones such as the "Kingcase" by Ronson. (Pictured in Plate # 113 of this book).

There are gentlemen's canes and walking sticks that contain lighters, cigar holders, a match safe and even a whistle! These items were made for those days when a gentleman wasn't completely dressed without the proper accessories.

A new chapter has been added on ashtrays. These are becoming a very popular and exciting collectable. Shown are just a sample of the different types made. From the rubber tires with metal or glass ashtrays to the popular chromium animal ones. Some have unique advertisements for different products, businesses, and places, while others like the ceramic bellhop held cigarettes.

Again we have included more magazine ads on lighters, tobacco products, and accessories for your enjoyment. There are humorous ads, but all are fun to see. Definitely something for everyone, whether you're a smoker or a collector!

Thank you to everyone who purchased the first book. We, along with the people of the Bridge Community in Denver, where the proceeds from the first book were donated, are grateful. I hope you enjoyed the book and am confident this one will be equally enjoyable!

— ADVERTISING —

Plate 1 • Chromium and enamel pocket lighter made by My-lite. Circa early 1980's. 2¼" H., 1½" W. $5.00 – 10.00.

Plate 2 • Painted metal Winston promotional table lighter made by GILLETT CO. Circa 1985. 4¼" H., 1¾" Dia. $5.00 – 10.00.

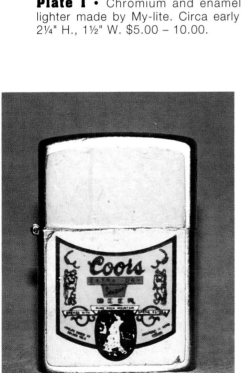

Plate 3 • Chromium lighter with advertising decal on front made by My-Lite. Circa mid 1960's. 2¼" H., 1½" W. $5.00 – 10.00.

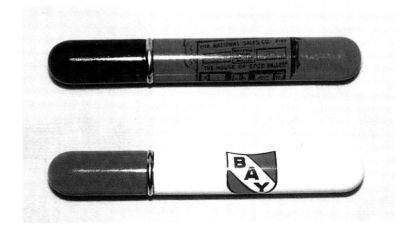

Plate 4 • Both tube-style chromium and enamel pocket lighters made by Redilite. Circa late 1940's. 3" H., ⅜" Dia. $15.00 – 20.00 each.

Plate 6 • Chromium and enamel pocket lighter made in Japan. Circa 1955. 1¾" H., 2" W. $15.00 – 20.00.

Plate 5 • Chromium pocket lighter made by Lansing. Circa 1975. 1¾" H., 2" W. $10.00 – 15.00.

Plate 7 • Brass pocket lighter with gift box made by Evans. Circa late 1930's. 2" H., 1½" W. $25.00 – 40.00.

Plate 8 • Chromium and painted pocket lighter made by Penguin. Circa late 1950's. 1¾" H., 2" W. $10.00 – 15.00.

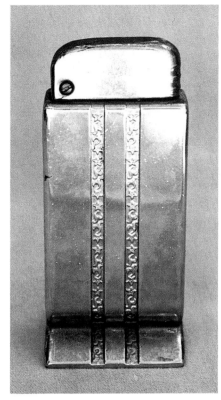

(Front)

Plate 9 • Chromium table lighter made by Bowers Mfg. Co. (showing advertisement on side). Circa late 1940's. 3½" H., 1¾" W. $20.00 – 30.00.

Plate 11 • Plastic butane pocket lighter made in Korea. Circa 1985. 3" H., 1" W. $5.00 – 10.00.

Plate 10 • Chromium and enamel pocket lighter made by BARLOW. Circa 1965. 2¼" H., 1½" W. $10.00 – 15.00.

Plate 12 • Both chromium and enamel tube-style pocket lighters made by Redilite. Circa late 1940's. 3" H., ⅜" Dia. $15.00 – 20.00 each.

Plate 13 • Painted metal table lighter that holds a disposable butane pocket lighter. Circa early 1970's. 3½" H., 1¾" Dia. $10.00 – 20.00.

Plate 14 • Chromium pocket lighter made by SUN. Circa mid 1950's. 2" H., 1½" W. $5.00 – 10.00.

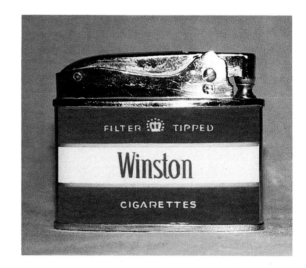

Plate 15 • Chromium pocket lighter made by Penguin. Circa early 1960's. 1¾" H., 2" W. $10.00 – 15.00.

Plate 16 • Chromium and painted tube-style pocket lighter made in Japan. Circa mid 1950's. 3⅛" H., ⅜" Dia. $10.00 – 20.00.

Plate 17 • Chromium pocket lighter with decals on the front and back made in Japan. Circa late 1960's. 2¼" H., 1½" W. $5.00 – 10.00.

Plate 18 • Brass lift-arm butane pocket lighter made in Korea. Circa mid 1970's. 2½" H., ¾" W. $10.00 – 20.00.

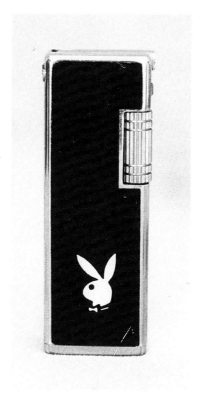

Plate 19 • Brass and enamel lift-arm butane pocket lighter made in Korea. Circa mid 1960's. 2½" H., ¾" W. $10.00 – 20.00.

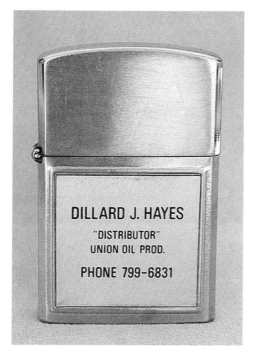

Plate 20 • Chromium pocket lighter made by BARLOW. Circa 1965. 2¼" H., 1½" W. $10.00 – 15.00.

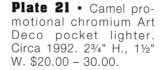

Plate 21 • Camel promotional chromium Art Deco pocket lighter. Circa 1992. 2¾" H., 1½" W. $20.00 – 30.00.

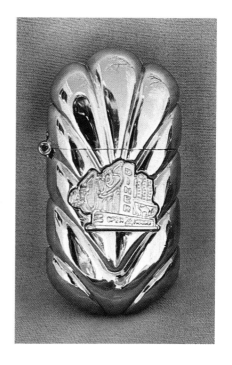

Plate 22 • Chromium and enamel pocket lighter made in Japan. Circa 1965. 1¾" H., 2" W. $10.00 – 20.00.

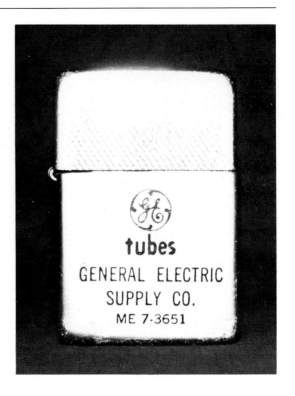

Plate 23 • Brass and enamel pocket lighter made by Park Industries. Circa late 1950's. 2¼" H., 1½" W. $10.00 – 20.00.

Plate 24 • Chromium and enamel pocket lighter by Vulcan. Circa mid 1960's. 1¾" H., 2" W. $15.00 – 20.00.

Plate 25 • Chromium pocket lighter made by Zeus. Circa late 1960's. 2¼" H., 1½" W. $10.00 – 15.00.

Plate 26 • Chromium pocket lighter with decals on front and back made in Japan. Circa early 1960's. 2¼" H., 1½" W. $10.00 – 15.00.

Plate 27 • Slim chromium and enamel pocket lighter made by Park Lighter Co. Circa mid 1960's. 2¼" H., 1" W. $10.00 – 15.00.

Plate 28 • Chromium and enamel pocket lighter made by BARLOW. Circa early 1960's. 2¼" H., 1½" W. $10.00 – 15.00.

Plate 29 • Chromium pocket lighter made by Zippo. Circa 1963. 2¼" H., 1¼" W. $10.00 – 15.00.

— ANIMALS —

Plate 30 • Brass wolf (dressed as a cowboy) striker lighter. Circa mid 1930's. 5½" H., 2" W. $225.00 – 275.00.

Plate 31 • Metal kangaroo made in Japan. Circa late 1960's. 3¾" H., 3½" W. $15.00 – 20.00.

Plate 32 • Painted metal Scottie dog made by Strikalite. Circa late 1930's. 2½" H., 3" W. $25.00 – 40.00.

Plate 33 • Metal camel made in Japan. Circa late 1940's. 2" H., 3" W. $15.00 – 25.00.

Plate 34 • Brass donkey made in Japan. Circa mid 1950's. 2" H., 2½" W. $15.00 – 20.00.

Plate 35 • Replica cigarette ad. Circa 1985. 3" H., 2" W. $3.00 – 5.00. Black cat butane pocket lighter made in France by Djeep Jr. Circa 1993. 2" H., 1" W. $3.00 – 5.00.

Plate 36 • Metal camel lighter and ashtray, made in Japan. Circa early 1960's. Ashtray 5" x 3½". Camel 3½" H., 4" W. $20.00 – 30.00.

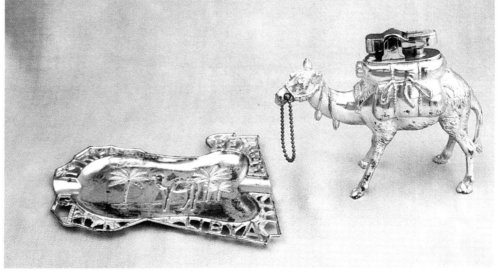

Plate 37 • Painted metal elephant made by Strikalite. Circa late 1940's. 3" H., 3½" W. $20.00 – 30.00.

Plate 38 • Metal bulldog made in Austria (head lifts up to reveal lighter). Dated April 2, 1912. 2¼" H., 2¾" W. $75.00 – 100.00.

Plate 39 • "Scotty" dog striker table lighter made of oxidized copper by Ronson. Circa 1936. 4" H., 5¾" W. $200.00 – 250.00.

Plate 40 • Another view of plate 39.

— ART DECO —

Plate 41 • Chrome and akro agate smoke stand with electric lighter, two ashtrays, and a covered cigarette receptacle. The base lights up for use at night. Circa mid 1930's. 27" H., 11" Dia at base. $125.00 – 175.00.

Plate 42 • Chrome and enamel ashtray stand. Circa late 1940's. 22" H., 8½" Dia. at base. $25.00 – 40.00.

Plate 43 • Chrome and akro agate smoking stand with electric lighter, ashtrays, and cigarette receptacle. The base lights up for night use. Circa mid 1930's. 27½" H., 12" Dia at base. $150.00 – 200.00.

Plate 44 • The "Spartan" chromium and enamel table lighter made by Ronson. Circa 1950. 2⅜" H., 3" W. $10.00 – 20.00.

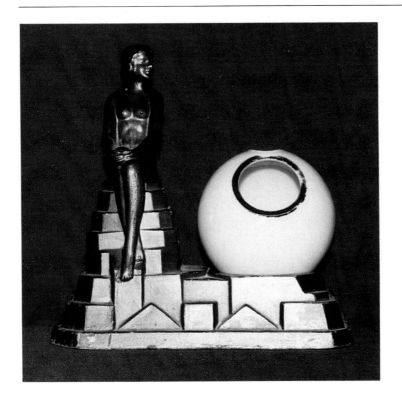

Plate 45 • Round glass ashtray on a metal base with a nude lady. Circa 1930. 6" H., 6¼" W. $75.00 – 100.00.

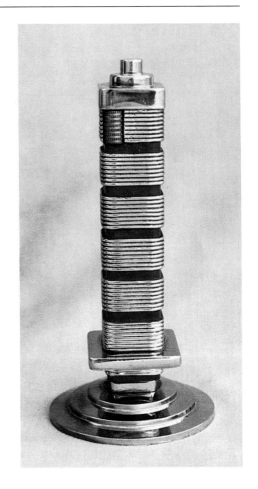

Plate 47 • Chrome and akro agate smoking stand with electric lighter, ashtrays, and cigarette receptacle. Base lights up for night use. Circa mid 1930's. 30" H., 11" Dia. at base. $125.00 – 175.00.

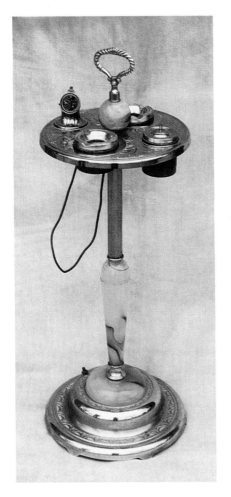

Plate 46 • The "Johnson Wax Tower" chromium and enamel table lighter. Circa 1930's. 5¾" H., 2¾" Dia. at base. $250.00 – 300.00.

Plate 48 • The "Lotus" 24K gold-plate and enamel table lighter made by Ronson. Circa 1953. 2¼" H., 3¼" W. $15.00 – 25.00.

Plate 49 • Wooden painted butler ashtray holder. Circa 1930's. 36" H., 10" W. at base. $50.00 – 100.00.

Plate 50 • Wooden painted butler ashtray holder. Circa 1930's. 31½" H., 10½" W. at base. $50.00 – 100.00.

Plate 51 • Statue of Liberty smoking stand with electric lighter, ashtrays, and cigarette receptacle. The torch lights up for use at night. Circa 1930's. 27" H., 10½" Dia. at base. $175.00 – 225.00.

— Ashtrays —

Plate 52 • Metal painted bellhop with ashtray on the base. Circa 1930's. 4¼" H., 4" W. at base. $50.00 – 75.00.

Plate 53 • Glass ashtray from the Denver Playboy Club. Circa 1960's. ½" H., 3¾" W. $10.00 – 20.00.

Plate 54 • Chrome cat ashtray. Circa 1938. 2½" H., 7¼" W. $20.00 – 40.00.

Plate 55 • Rubber tire with metal ashtray. Circa 1920's. 1" H., 4⅜" Dia. $50.00 – 70.00.

Plate 57 • Chrome alligator ashtray. Circa 1936. 1½" H., 4½" Dia. $20.00 – 30.00.

Plate 56 • Rubber tire with glass ashtray. Circa 1930's. 1" H., 6½" Dia. $45.00 – 65.00.

Plate 58 • Rubber tire with glass advertisement ashtray. Circa 1950's. 1½" H., 5½" W. $30.00 – 50.00.

Plate 59 • Painted ceramic bellhop ashtray and cigarette holder. Circa late 1930's. 4½" H., 4" W. $40.00 – 60.00.

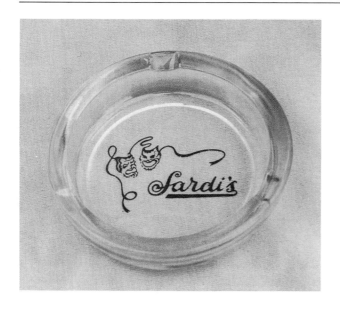

Plate 60 • Glass ashtray from Sardi's Restaurant in New York. Circa early 1980's. ¾" H., 3¾" Dia. $10.00 – 20.00.

Plate 61 • Rubber tire with metal advertising ashtray for Firestone Truck Tires. Circa 1920's. 2" H., 4¼" Dia. $75.00 – 100.00.

Plate 62 • Rubber tire and glass ashtray. Circa 1930's. 1½" H., 6½" Dia. $75.00 – 100.00.

Plate 63 • Chrome pelican ashtray. Circa 1936. 1¾" H., 4½" Dia. $20.00 – 30.00.

Plate 64 • Closed view of a brass pocket ashtray with a painted cigarette on the lid. Circa 1950's. ½" H., 2¼" W. $10.00 – 15.00.

Plate 65 • Open view of Plate 64.

Plate 66 • Rubber tire with glass ashtray that has a built in match-book holder. Circa 1930's. 1½" H., 7" Dia. $70.00 – 100.00.

Plate 67 • Rubber tire with an akro agate ashtray. Circa early 1930's. 1½" H., 6¼" Dia. $65.00 – 85.00.

Plate 68 • Rubber tire and glass ashtray with a built in matchbook holder. Circa 1930's. 1¼" H., 5¼" Dia. $70.00 – 100.00.

Plate 69 • Rubber tire and glass ashtray. Circa early 1940's. 1¼" H., 6" Dia. $50.00 – 75.00.

— BEYOND THE ORDINARY —

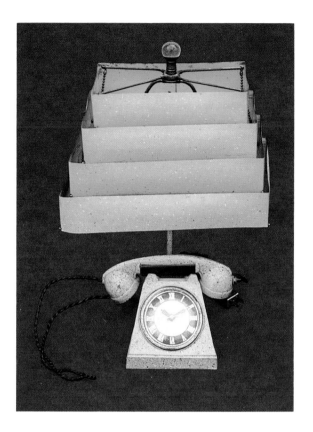

Plate 70 • Electric telephone table lighter with a clock and lamp made by the TREA-BOYE Corp. (lighter located in the mouth piece of the phone receiver). Circa late 1930's. 16½" H., 5" W. at base. $90.00 – 120.00.

Plate 71 • Chromium and Bakelite hula dancer (uses batteries and fluid) made by Arrow Products Mfg. Co. (The skirt is spring loaded and opens in the front.) Circa late 1930's. 5¾" H., 4" Dia. at base. $50.00 – 75.00.

Plate 72 • Electric lamp socket table lighter. Circa 1940's. 4" H., 2" Dia. at base. $40.00 – 60.00.

Plate 73 • Ceramic electric table lighter made by MacDonald Specialties. Circa late 1930's. 2½" H., 3¼" Dia. at base. $50.00 – 70.00.

Plate 74 • Bottom view of the previous plate showing original label.

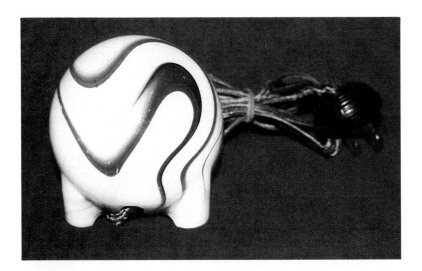

Plate 76 • Round electric table lighter made of akro agate. Circa mid 1930's. 2¾" Dia. $35.00 – 50.00.

Plate 75 • Chromium and enamel table lighter made by Silent Flame (uses fluid and batteries). Circa 1940's. 3¾" H., 2⅝" Dia. at base. $25.00 – 40.00.

Plate 77 • Brass electric table lighter with heating element in the mouth. Circa 1920's. 7" H., 3¾" Dia. at base. $125.00 – 200.00.

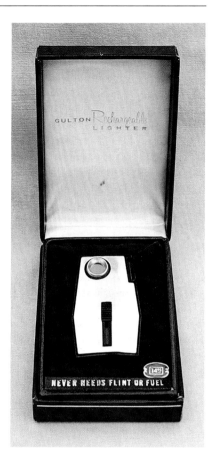

Plate 78 • Rechargeable electric pocket lighter. Sold new for $14.95 (just plug into a regular household outlet to charge), made by Gulton. Circa late 1950's. 2¾" H., 1½" W. $50.00 – 75.00.

Plate 79 • Electric nickel-plated table lighter with heating element in the lady's mouth. Circa 1920's. 7¼" H., 4½" Dia. at base. $175.00 – 250.00.

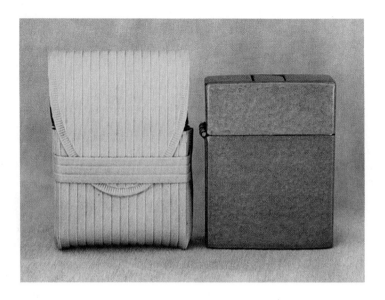

Plate 80 • Spy camera lighter with case. The camera really works with a split roll of 35mm film made by CAMERA-LITE. Circa 1940's. 2¼" H., 1¾" W. $300.00 – 500.00.

Plate 81 • Open view of Plate 80 showing the view finder (in the lid), lens (on the bottom half of the lighter), the shutter release (on the top), and the wheel to advance the film.

— CIGARETTE CASES —

Plate 83 • Chromium and tortoise enamel "Sportcase" made by Ronson. Circa 1936. 4⅛" H., 2" W. $50.00 – 70.00.

Plate 82 • The "Pal" chromium and burgundy enamel made by Ronson. Circa 1941. 4⅛" H., 2" W. $50.00 – 80.00.

Plate 84 • Gold-plate lighter/case made by Evans. Circa mid 1930's. 4¼" H., 2½" W. $50.00 – 75.00.

Plate 85 • Chromium and tortoise enamel lighter/case made by Evans. Circa 1928. 4¼" H., 2⅛" W. $70.00 – 100.00.

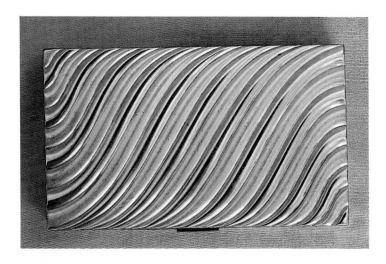

Plate 86 • Gold-plated ladies' compact and cigarette case made by Evans. Circa mid 1930's. 5½" H., 3⅛" W. $100.00 – 150.00.

Plate 87 • Chromium lighter/case made by Royal Case-lite. (When the case is closed the lighter automatically lights.) Circa 1940's. 4⅜" H., 3⅛" W. $60.00 – 80.00.

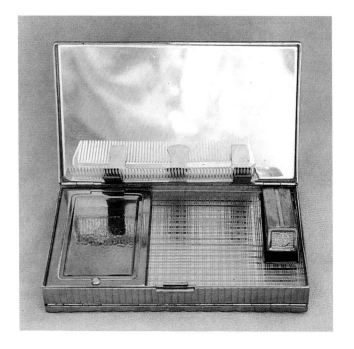

Plate 88 • Opened view of Plate 86 to show comb (center), make-up compact (left side), and lip stick tube (on the right).

Plate 89 • Bottom view of Plate 86 to show where the cigarettes fit.

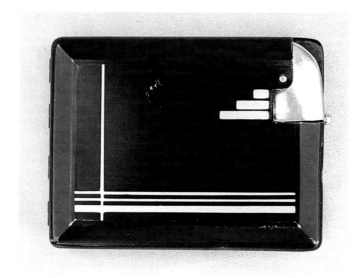

Plate 90 • Chromium and enamel lighter/case made by Magic Case Mfg. (when the side mechanism is pushed forward it automatically lights the cigarette and slides it out of the case). Circa mid 1930's. 4¼" H., 3⅛" W. $75.00 – 100.00.

Plate 91 • Opened view of Plate 90 showing the spring that holds the cigarettes in place and the way the lit cigarette comes out.

Plate 93 • Opened view of Plate 92 to show the make-up compartment and mirror. The cigarettes were placed behind the mirror.

Plate 92 • Chromium and enamel ladies' lighter/case/compact made by Evans. Circa early 1930's. 4" H., 2" W. $80.00 – 110.00.

Plate 94 • Ladies' brass case (with marble-like material on the lid). Made by Marhill of New York. Circa early 1950's. 5¼" H., 2⅛" W. $45.00 – 60.00.

Plate 95 • Opened view of Plate 94 to show the lighter. The lighter pops up when the case is opened.

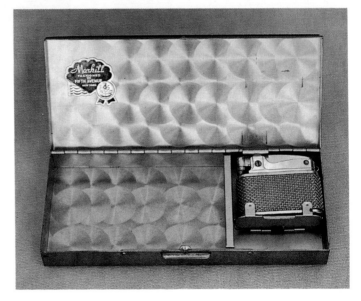

Plate 96 • Sterling silver cigarette case. Circa mid 1930's. 3½" H., 2¼" W. $75.00 – 100.00.

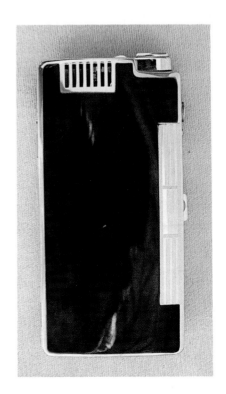

Plate 97 • The "Pal" chromium and tortoise enamel lighter/case made by Ronson. Circa 1941. 4⅛" H., 2" W. $50.00 – 80.00.

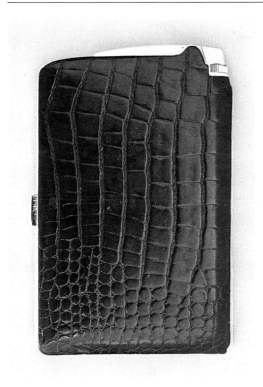

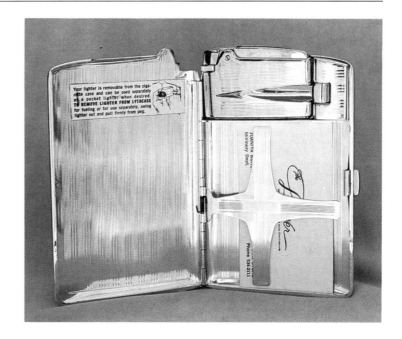

Plate 99 • Open view of Plate 98 to show the inside compartment and removable lighter.

Plate 98 • Chromium and leather "Lytacase" with a removable butane "Adonis" lighter made by Ronson. Circa late 1950's. 5" H., 3¼" W. $50.00 – 75.00.

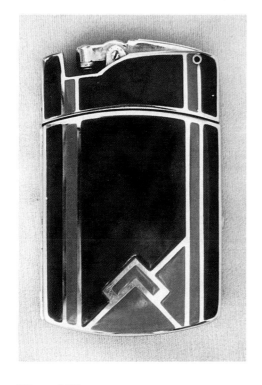

Plate 101 • Gold-plate and tortoise enamel lighter/case with gift box made by Marathon. Circa mid 1930's. 4⅛" H., 2⅝" W. $100.00 – 125.00.

Plate 100 • The "Tuxedo" in chromium and two shades of enamel made by Ronson. Circa 1930. 4⅛" H., 2⅝" W. $75.00 – 100.00.

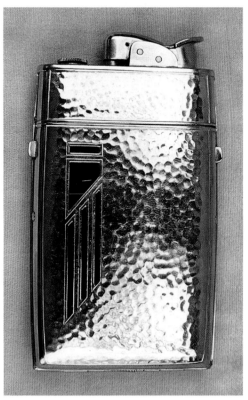

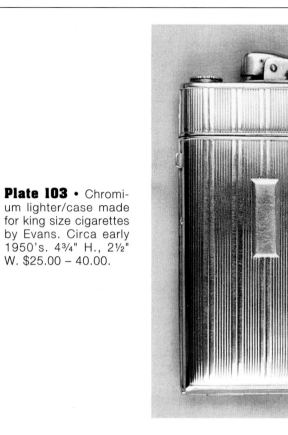

Plate 103 • Chromium lighter/case made for king size cigarettes by Evans. Circa early 1950's. 4¾" H., 2½" W. $25.00 – 40.00.

Plate 102 • Chromium and enamel lighter/case made by Evans. Circa late 1930's. 4¼" H., 2½" W. $25.00 – 40.00.

Plate 105 • Open view of Plate 104 showing mirror and make-up compartment.

Plate 104 • Chromium and enamel lighter/case/compact made by Evans. (Note: due to the compact the case only held seven cigarettes.) Circa early 1930's. 4¼" H., 2½" W. $100.00 – 125.00.

Plate 106 • Close up view of the compact lid from Plate 104.

Plate 107 • Ladies' embroidered silk cigarette purse with brass lighter attached by a chain made by Fashion Company. Circa early 1950's. Purse 4¼" H., 3" W.; lighter 1⅜" H., 1⅛" W. $40.00 – 60.00.

Plate 108 • "Lektrocase" chromium and wooden slats cigarette lighter/case made by Glolite Corp. To use the lighter the cigarette is inserted into the hole (top, right side of case). Circa mid 1930's. 3" H., 3⅞" W. $80.00 – 100.00.

Plate 109 • Open view of Plate 108 to show where cigarette compartment is. The wooden slats slide around to the back of the case to open.

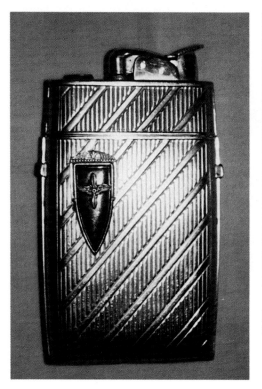

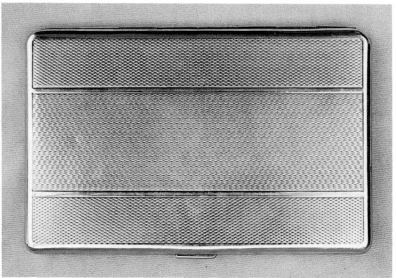

Plate 111 • Chromium cigarette case lined in brass made by Kincraft in England. Circa late 1940's. 5¼" H., 3⅜" W. $45.00 – 65.00.

Plate 110 • Chromium lighter/case with the U.S. Army Air Corp's emblem in blue enamel with gold trim made by Evans. Circa early 1940's. 4¼" H., 2½" W. $75.00 – 100.00.

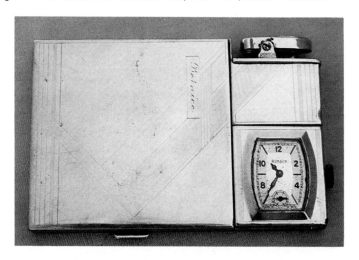

Plate 113 • The "Kingcase" dureum finish lighter/case made by Ronson. (Note the small second hand on the watch.) Circa 1936. 2⅞" H., 4⅜" W. $300.00 – 400.00.

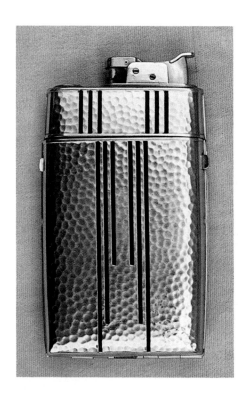

Opened view of plate 113.

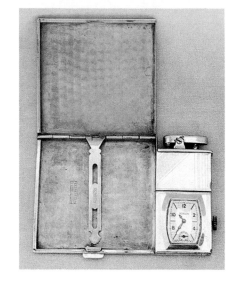

Plate 112 • Chromium and enamel lighter/case made by Evans. Circa early 1930's. 4¼" H., 2½" W. $40.00 – 60.00.

— DECORATIVE —

Plate 115 • The "Corinthian" table lighter made by Zippo. Circa 1960. 3⅞" H., 2¼" Dia. $25.00 – 40.00.

Plate 114 • Brass and ceramic table lighter made by Evans. Circa late 1930's. 6½" H., 3¼" Dia. at base. $30.00 – 50.00.

Plate 116 • Chromium and green and black enamel table top cigarette holder made by Park Sherman. Circa late 1930's. (To open the top compartment rolls back.) 2½" H., 3¾" W. $30.00 – 50.00 each. (See plate 117 different color.)

Plate 117 • Same as Plate 116 except for the color.

Plate 118 • The "Decor" made by Ronson. (The plastic cover can be removed to change the fabric to match your decor.) Circa 1954. 2¾" H., 4¼" Dia. $20.00 – 35.00.

Plate 119 • The "Cupid" table lighter made by Ronson. This lighter has three gold cherubs on black enamel. Circa 1956. 2¼" H., 1¾" Dia. $25.00 – 40.00.

Plate 120 • The "Minerva" table lighter made by Ronson. This lighter is ivory porcelain with a floral pattern, the top and base are silver plate. Circa 1952. 3" H., 2¾" W. $30.00 – 50.00.

Plate 121 • Marble base with gold-plated lighter made by Alfred Dunhill. Circa 1955. 2½" H., 3¾" W. $250.00 – 300.00.

Plate 122 • Small ceramic table lighter made in France. Top comes off to reveal the lighter. Circa late 1950's. 2½" H., 1¼" W. $20.00 – 30.00.

Plate 123 • Marble base with brass lighter made by Evans. Circa late 1930's. 3¾" H., 2⅛" Dia. at base. $25.00 – 30.00

Plate 124 • Lift-arm table lighter made by Fay Mfg. Co. The base has a nude woman with a clock. Patented March 29, 1927. 6¾" H., 3" W. at base. $80.00 – 120.00.

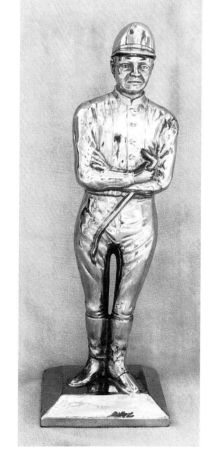

Plate 125 • Chromium Jockey. Circa early 1950's. (The back of his cap is hinged to operate lighter.) 8½" H., 2⅞" W. at base. $150.00 – 200.00.

Plate 126 • Chromium table lighter with gold trim made by Prince. Circa mid 1950's. 2⅝" H., 2¼" W. at base. $15.00 – 25.00.

Plate 127 • Gold-plated table lighter made by Evans. Circa early 1930's. 3⅝" H., 2½" W. $60.00 – 80.00.

Plate 128 • Pipe, chromium table lighter with etched wooden base made by Albert. Circa 1950's. 2⅜" H., 4½" W. $25.00 – 40.00.

Plate 129 • Brass globe table lighter made in Japan. Circa early 1960's. 3¼" H., 2" Dia. at base. $15.00 – 25.00.

Plate 131 • Gold-plated table lighter made by Evans. Circa early 1930's. 3⅝" H., 2½" W. $50.00 – 70.00.

Plate 130 • Bronze finished golf caddy. (The bag comes off the base and the handle, where the clubs are operates the lighter.) Circa early 1930's. Caddy 7" H., 4¼" W. at base; bag 4¾" H., 1⅜" W. $250.00 – 300.00.

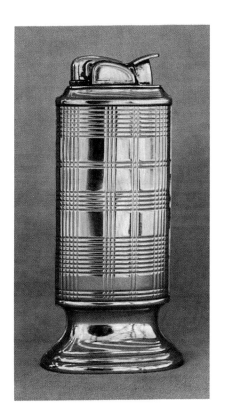

Plate 132 • A unique gold-plated table lighter made by Evans. Circa 1930's. 4¾" H., 2¼" W. $60.00 – 80.00.

Plate 133 • Silver-plated "Juno" table lighter made by Ronson. Circa 1952. 6¼" H., 2" Dia. at base. $30.00 – 50.00.

— MATCHES —

Matchbooks from different parts of the country and businesses. All circa 1940's. All $3.00 – 5.00.

Plate 134

Plate 135

Plate 136

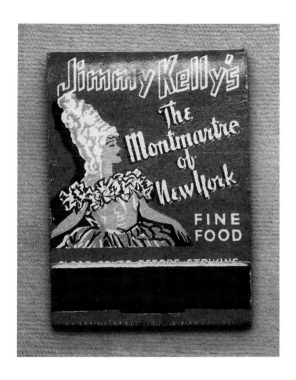

Plate 137

Plate 138

Plate 139

Plate 140

Plate 141

Plate 142

Plate 143

Plate 144

Plate 145

Plate 146

Plate 147

Plate 148

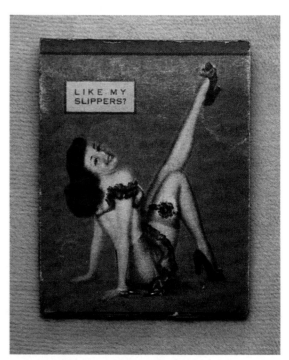

Plate 149

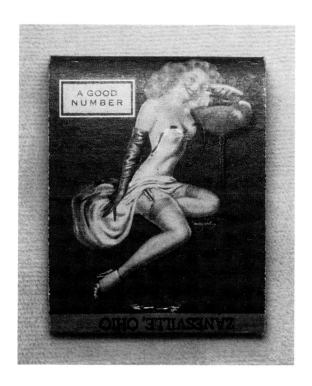

Plate 150

Plate 151

Plate 152

Plate 153

Plate 154 • Plastic butane spark plug pocket lighter with key chain made by P.L.A. Circa early 1990's. 3" H., ¾" Dia. $5.00 – 10.00.

Plate 155 • Chromium and enamel boat motor made by SWANK. Circa early 1960's. 5" H., 2⅜" W. $50.00 – 90.00.

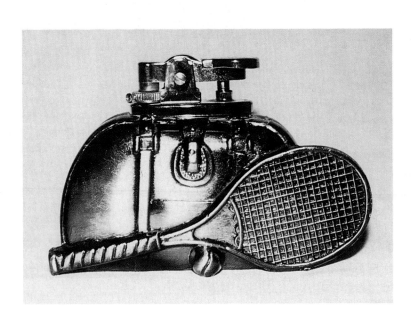

Plate 156 • Chromium butane tennis racquet with gym bag table lighter made in Japan. Circa early 1990's. 2⅜" H., 3⅞" W. $15.00 – 25.00.

Plate 157 • Plastic butane ice skate from Germany. Circa early 1990's. 1⅝" H., 2½" W. $15.00 – 25.00.

Plate 158 • Brass and leather bellows. Circa mid 1960's. Lighter is operated by squeezing the handles together. 2" H., 7¼" W. $20.00 – 30.00.

Plate 160 • Metal boot lighter (lever on the back of the boot opens the lighter). Circa 1920's. 1¾" H., 2⅝" W. $60.00 – 100.00.

Plate 159 • Plastic torpedo-shaped pocket lighter. Circa late 1930's. 3⅛" H., ⅝" Dia. $15.00 – 25.00.

Plate 161 • Metal and enamel tube-style pocket lighter made by BALLoFLINT. Circa late 1940's. 3" H., ⅝" Dia. $10.00 – 20.00.

Plate 162 • Plastic butane music note from Germany. Circa early 1990's. 2" H., 1⅝" W. $15.00 – 25.00.

Plate 163 • Plastic and metal striker-type pocket lighter. Circa late 1980's. 2" H., 1¼" W. $5.00 – 10.00.

Plate 164 • Squeeze handle butane pocket lighter from Germany. Circa late 1980's. 3" H., 1¼" W. $10.00 – 20.00.

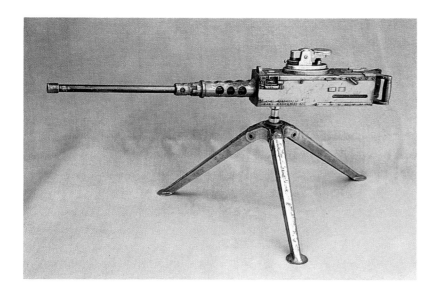

Plate 165 • Chromium and metal butane machine gun mounted on a tripod. Circa mid 1980's. 5½" H., 11⅞" W. $35.00 – 50.00.

Plate 166 • Plastic butane canteen pocket lighter from Germany (cap comes off to reveal lighter). Circa late 1980's. 2¼" H., 1⅜" W. $ 15.00 – 25.00.

Plate 168 • Brass table lighter shaped like a bomb. Circa early 1930's. 4" H., 1¼" Dia. $40.00 – 60.00.

Plate 167 • Metal and enamel tube-style pocket lighter made by BALLoFLINT. Circa late 1940's. 2⅝" H., ½" Dia. $10.00 – 20.00.

Plate 169 • Limited edition lighter and knife set made by Zippo and Case. Circa 1993. Lighter 2¼" H., 1½" W.; knife opened 1¼" H., 8⅜" W. $400.00 – 500.00.

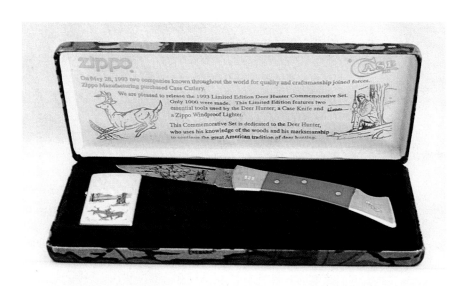

Plate 170 • Lighter and knife from Plate 169 in gift box.

Plate 171 • Disposable butane pocket lighter in a metal holder with a crest that has the Eiffel Tower and the word Paris on it. Circa early 1990's. 3¼" H., 1" W. $5.00 – 10.00.

— OCCUPIED JAPAN —

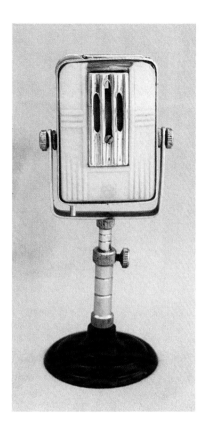

Plate 174 • Chromium and mother-of-pearl lift-arm pocket lighter made in Occupied Japan. Circa 1948. 1⅞" H., 1⅝" W. $75.00 – 100.00.

Plate 172 • Silver-plated cowboy made in Occupied Japan. Head is hinged in the back to reveal the lighter. Circa 1948. 4" H., 1¾" W. $75.00 – 100.00.

Plate 173 • Chromium and plastic microphone made in Occupied Japan. Circa late 1940's. 4⅞" H., 1⅞" W. $125.00 – 150.00.

Plate 175 • Chromium and ceramic elephant table lighter made in Occupied Japan. Circa 1948. 3½" H., 4" W. $60.00 – 90.00.

Plate 176 • Silver-plated cowboy boot with a sunburst on the front and floral design on the back made in Occupied Japan. (This boot was made without a spur.) Circa 1950. 2⅞" H., 2⅞" W. $40.00 – 60.00.

Plate 177 • Chromium typewriter made in Occupied Japan. (Lights by pressing space bar.) Circa 1948. 1¾" H., 3½" W. $125.00 – 150.00.

Plate 178 • Silver-plated bellhop with suitcase made in Occupied Japan. (Pick up the lighter and it automatically lights, the flame comes out of the top of suitcase.) Circa 1948. 4½" H., 3½" W. $150.00 – 200.00.

Plate 179 • Sewing machine with plastic cigarette holder in the base made in Occupied Japan. (Lights by the needle.) 3" H., 4" W. $125.00 – 150.00.

Plate 180 • Silver-plated barrel table lighter made in Occupied Japan. Circa 1948. 3⅛" H., 1¾" Dia. $40.00 – 60.00.

— POCKET LIGHTERS —

Plate 181 • Very unique pocket lighter that has a pull out wick on a chain and another in the cap that unscrews. (Supposedly the city of St. Louis gave the lighters to all the soldiers in the 35th Division who fought in France.) Circa 1918. 3¼" H., 2" W. $200.00 – 300.00.

Plate 182 • Back view of plate 181.

Plate 183 • The "Trickette" brass and rhinestone pocket lighter made by Wisner. Circa early 1950's. 1½" H., 1¾" W. $25.00 – 40.00.

Plate 184 • Chromium pocket lighter with a unique floral design made by Evans. Circa late 1940's. 2" H., 1½" W. $25.00 – 40.00.

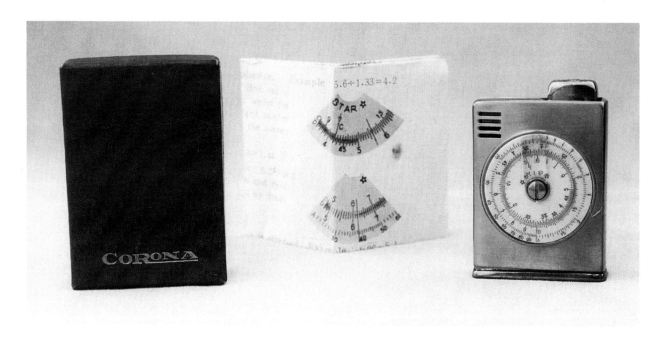

Plate 185 • The "Renown" pocket lighter made by Corona. This lighter has a built-in slide rule on the front. Shown with the instructions and gift box. Circa 1945. 2¼" H., 1½" W. $100.00 – 125.00.

Plate 186 • Chromium lift-arm pocket lighter made by Colibri. Circa 1928. 2" H., 1⅝" W. $150.00 – 200.00.

Plate 187 • Brass lighter with ostrich hide band made by Elgin American. Circa early 1950's. 1¾" H., 1⅜" W. $25.00 – 40.00.

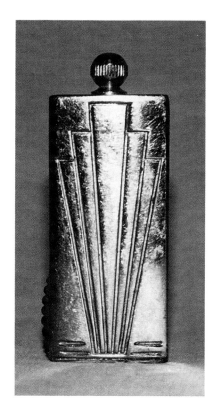

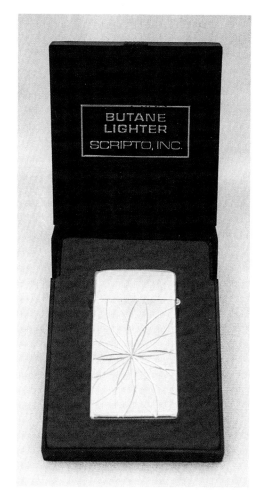

Plate 189 • Brass butane lighter in gift box made by Scripto. Circa late 1950's. 2½" H., 1¼" W. $20.00 – 35.00.

Plate 188 • Chromium striker-type pocket lighter made by Match King. Circa late 1940's. 2⅝" H., 1" W. $15.00 – 25.00.

Plate 190 • Chromium butane pocket lighter made by Colibri in Ireland. Circa early 1960's. 3" H., ⅞" W. $50.00 – 75.00.

Plate 191 • Ladies' brass and leather covered pocket lighter made in Germany. Circa mid 1950's. 1⅜" H., 1½" W. $25.00 – 40.00.

Plate 192 • Leather flap of Plate 191 opened to view lighter.

Plate 193 • Chromium butane pocket pipe lighter made by Colibri. (Bottom of lighter has a tobacco tamper.) Circa late 1960's. 3¼" H., ½" Dia. at base. $20.00 – 40.00.

Plate 194 • Small brass lighter made in Japan. Circa 1950's. 1⅛" H., ⅝" W. $5.00 – 10.00.

Plate 195 • Chromium pocket lighter made by Gibson. Circa mid 1950's. 1¾" H., 2⅛" W. $15.00 – 25.00.

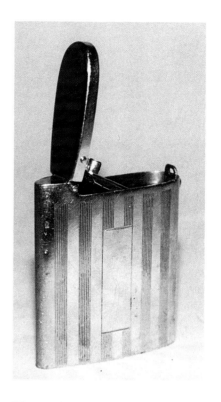

Plate 196 • Platinum plate pocket lighter made by Lektrolite. Circa late 1930's. 1¾" H., 1⅝" W. $20.00 – 30.00.

Plate 197 • D-Day Commemorative lighter in black finish with gift tin made by Zippo. Circa 1994. Lighter 2¼" H., 1½" W; tin 2" H., 4¼" Dia. $20.00 – 40.00.

Plate 198 • The "Director" chromium pocket lighter made by Berkley. Circa late 1940's. 1¾" H., 2⅛" W. $25.00 – 40.00.

Plate 199 • Goldtone musical pocket lighter made by Crown. Circa late 1940's. 2⅝" H., 1⅜" W. $20.00 – 40.00.

Plate 200 • Brass pocket lighter with leather band made by Evans. Circa late 1940's. 2½" H., 1½" W. $25.00 – 40.00.

Plate 201 • Silver-plate with goldtone etched wheat design made by Zippo. Circa 1994. 2¼" H., 1½" W. $20.00 – 30.00.

Plate 202 • Silhouette of a lady on a chromium lighter made by Zippo. Circa 1994. 2¼" H., 1½" W. $10.00 – 20.00.

Plate 203 • The Zippo Lady etched on a chromium lighter made by Zippo. Circa 1993. 2¼" H., 1½" W. $15.00 – 25.00.

Plate 204 • The Zippo Lady in enamel on a chromium pocket lighter made by Zippo. (The Zippo lady is circa 1935.) Lighter circa 1993. 2¼" H., 1½" W. $15.00 – 25.00.

Plate 205 • The Zippo Lady etched on a chromium pocket lighter made by Zippo to remember their 5th anniversary (1932 – 1937). Circa 1993. 2¼" H., 1½" W. $20.00 – 30.00.

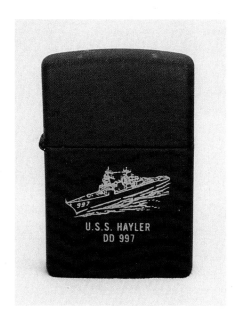

Plate 206 • Battle Ship U.S.S Hayler DD 997 chromium pocket lighter made by Zippo. Circa 1994. 2¼" H., 1½" W. $20.00 – 30.00 each.

Plate 207 • Same as Plate 206 except in a matte black finish.

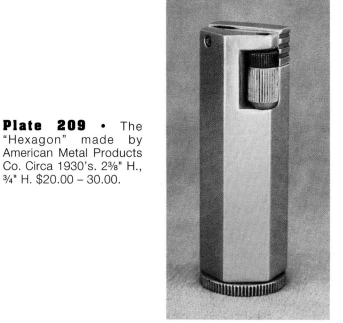

Plate 209 • The "Hexagon" made by American Metal Products Co. Circa 1930's. 2⅜" H., ¾" H. $20.00 – 30.00.

Plate 208 • Same as Plate 206 and 207 except in a brass finish.

Plate 210 • Chromium lift-arm pocket lighter made by TEE-VEE. Circa mid 1930's. 2¼" H., 1" W. $15.00 – 25.00.

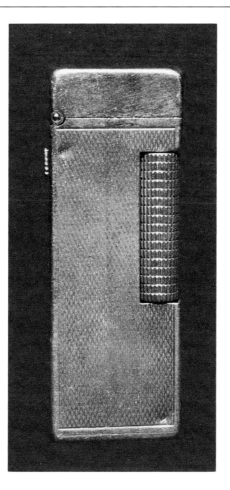

Plate 211 • Gold-plated butane lift-arm pocket lighter made by Dunhill in Switzerland. Circa mid 1950's. 2½" H., ⅞" W. $225.00 – 300.00.

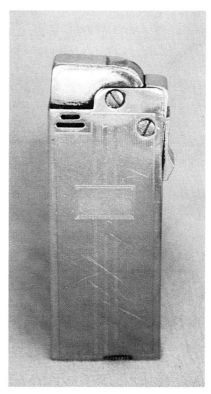

Plate 212 • Chromium lighter with a unique thumb slide action lever on the side to operate made by Thorens in Switzerland. Circa late 1940's. 2⅝" H., 1" W. $75.00 – 100.00.

Plate 213 • Chromium butane lighter made by Citation. Circa late 1950's. 1¼" H., 2¼" W. $20.00 – 30.00.

Plate 214 • Silver-plated lift-arm pocket lighter made by Evans. Circa late 1920's. 1⅞" H., 1½" W. $75.00 – 100.00.

Plate 215 • The "Princess" chromium with a leather band made by Ronson. Circa 1950's. 1⅞" H., 1½" W. $25.00 – 40.00.

Plate 216 • Chromium pistol with mother-of-pearl grips made in Japan. Circa early 1950's. 1½" H., 2" W. $25.00 – 40.00.

Plate 217 • Commemorative pocket lighter of the United States of America's 200th Birthday made by Storm King. Circa 1976. 2¼" H., 1¼" W. $15.00 – 20.00.

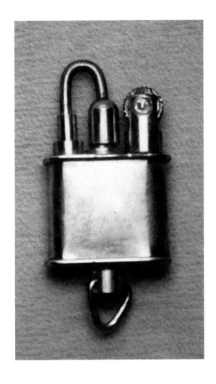

Plate 218 • Small brass lighter with a spring loaded wick snuffer that pivots. Circa early 1920's. 1¼" H., ⅝" W. $80.00 – 100.00.

Plate 219 • Same as plate 218 showing lighter ready to light.

Plate 220 • Chromium Swiss-made pocket lighter by Thorens. Circa early 1920's. 2¼" H., 1⅝" W. $45.00 – 60.00.

Plate 221 • Chromium butane pocket lighter made by Bentley in Austria. Circa late 1950's. 2¼" H., 1½" W. $20.00 – 40.00.

Plate 222 • Chromium and enamel lighter made by Imaco. Circa late 1950's. 2¼" H., 1½" W. $20.00 – 30.00.

Plate 223 • Chromium lift-arm pocket lighter made by Paramount. Circa mid 1920's. 1¾" H., 1½" W. $45.00 – 60.00.

Plate 224 • Chromium lift-arm pocket lighter that has a unique built-in wind-screen made by Polo in England. Circa mid 1930's. 2" H., 1⅝" W. $80.00 – 100.00.

Plate 225 • Chromium "Trig-A-Lite" pocket lighter made by Evans. Circa 1928. 2" H., 1½" W. $70.00 – 90.00.

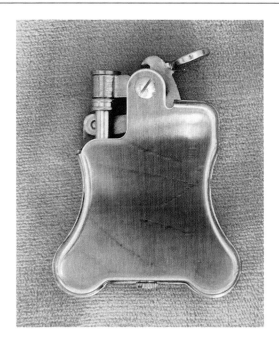

Plate 226 • Reproduction of Ronson's "Banjo" pocket lighter in chromium finish. Circa 1960's. 2⅜" H., 1⅞" W. $40.00 – 60.00.

Plate 227 • Reproduction of Ronson's "Banjo" pocket lighter with brass finish. Circa 1960's. 2⅜" H., 1⅞" W. $40.00 – 60.00.

Plate 228 • Chromium foxhole-style pocket lighter. Circa early 1940's. 2½" H., ⅞" W. $20.00 – 30.00.

Plate 229 • Same as previous Ronson "Banjo" pocket lighters except brass with floral design.

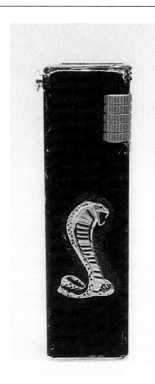

Plate 230 • Gold-plated and enamel butane pocket lighter made by Colibri. Circa mid 1970's. 2½" H., ¾" W. $30.00 – 50.00.

Plate 231 • Chromium butane pipe lighter made by Savinelli. Circa mid 1970's. 2¾" H., 1⅛" W. $25.00 – 40.00.

Plate 232 • Chromium and paint butane pocket lighter with a cobra snake on the front made by Cobid. Circa late 1960's. 2½" H., ⅝" W. $30.00 – 45.00.

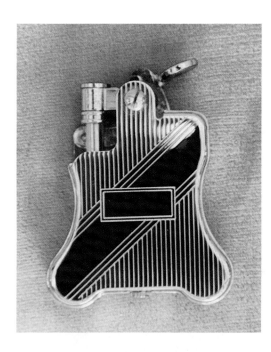

Plate 233 • Reproduction of Ronson's "Banjo" lighter in gold-plate and enamel finish. Circa 1960's. 2⅜" H., 1⅞" W. $60.00 – 80.00.

Plate 234 • Same as Plate 233 with brushed chromium finish.

Plate 236 • Small chromium lift-arm lighter made by Golden Wheel. Circa late 1940's. 1" H., ⅞" W. $20.00 – 30.00.

Plate 235 • Same as Plates 233 and 234 with a different gold-plate and enamel finish.

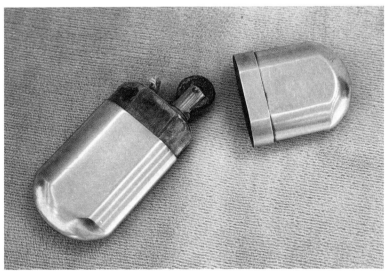

Plate 237 • Chromium finish pocket lighter made by Evans. Circa late 1940's. 2" H., 1½" W. $20.00 – 40.00.

Plate 238 • Brass replica pocket lighter. Circa late 1970's. 2¾" H., 1¼" W. $15.00 – 20.00.

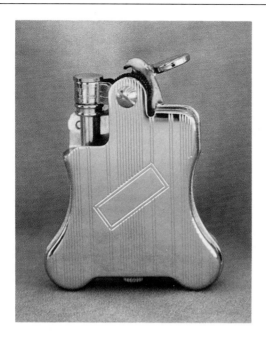

Plate 239 • Ronson's "Banjo" reproduction pocket lighter in gold-plated finish. Circa 1960's. 2⅜" H., 1⅞" W. $60.00 – 80.00.

Plate 240 • Same as Plate 239 in chromium finish.

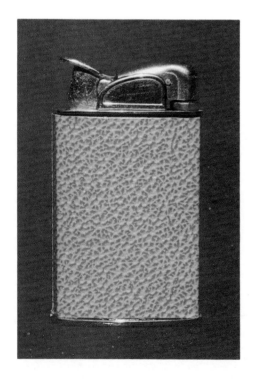

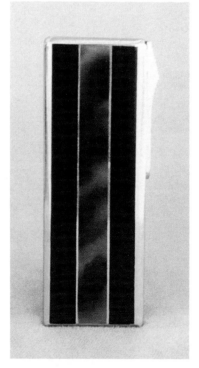

Plate 241 • Brass lighter with a leather band made by Evans. Circa late 1940's. 2½" H., 1½" W. $25.00 – 40.00.

Plate 242 • Brass and enamel butane pocket lighter made by Battat. Circa late 1970's. 2⅞" H., 1⅛" W. $15.00 – 25.00.

Plate 243 • Small chromium butane pocket lighter with a floral design made by Flamex. Circa 1970's. 1¾" H., 1" W. $15.00 – 20.00.

Plate 244 • Chromium foxhole-style lighter. Circa early 1940's. 1⅞" H., ¾" W. $20.00 – 30.00.

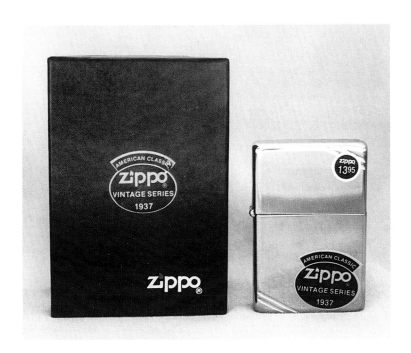

Plate 245 • Chromium Vintage series 1937 made by Zippo. Circa 1993. 2¼" H., 1½" W. $10.00 – 20.00.

Plate 246 • Chromium pocket lighter made by Goldwyn. Circa late 1950's. 1⅜" H., 1⅝" W. $10.00 – 20.00.

Plate 247 • Gold-plated pocket lighter with a watch, Swiss made. Circa 1960's. 2⅜" H., 1⅛" W. $60.00 – 80.00.

Plate 248 • Chromium pocket lighter with gift box made by Spark. Circa late 1950's. 2" H., 1¾" W. $20.00 – 30.00.

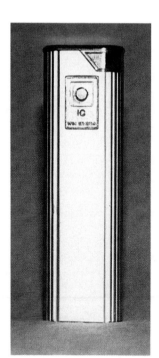

Plate 249 • The "Win Sensor" chromium butane pocket lighter made by IC. Circa late 1970's. 3¼" H., 1" W. $15.00 – 25.00.

Plate 250 • The Zippo American Eagle in chromium finish. (Each lighter has been individually numbered.) Circa 1994. 2¼" H., 1½" W. $15.00 – 25.00.

Plate 251 • The "Sport" chromium and leather lighter in a gift box made by Ronson. Circa 1956. 2" H., 1¾" W. $10.00 – 20.00.

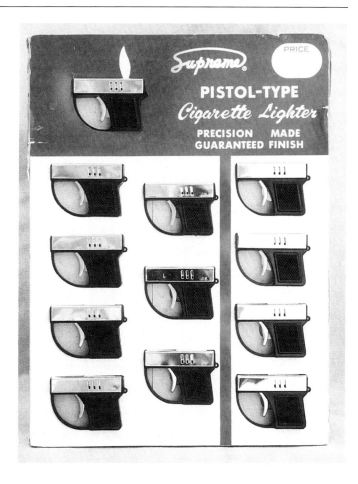

Plate 252 • Chromium and plastic gun lighters on a display board made by Supreme. Circa late 1950's. Gun 1½" H., 2¼" W.; display 12" H., 9" W. $90.00 – 100.00 (for display and guns).

Plate 253 • The "Vara Flame" chromium butane pocket lighter with gift box made by Ronson in England. Circa early 1960's. 2¾" H., 1" Dia. at base. $15.00 – 25.00.

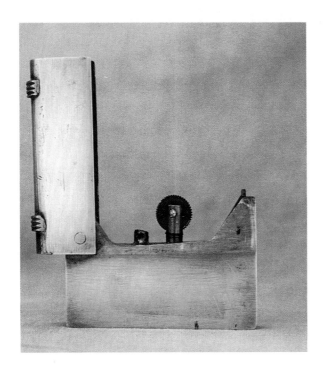

Plate 254 • Open view of brass pocket lighter shaped like a book. Circa 1918. 2½" H., 1¾" W. $75.00 – 100.00.

Plate 255 • Closed view of lighter in Plate 254.

Plate 256 • Zippo's D-Day Allied Heroes Collectors Edition set in a tin. This set has four brass finished lighters with a key chain in the center. Circa 1994. Lighters 2¼" H., 1½" W.; key chain 1¼" Dia.; tin 2" H., 8" Dia. $80.00 – 100.00.

Plate 257 • Close-up view of lighter in Plate 256. (General B.L. Montgomery.)

Plate 258 • Close-up view of lighter in Plate 256. (General Omar Bradley.)

Plate 259 • Close-up view of lighter in Plate 256. (General Dwight D. Eisenhower.)

Plate 260 • Close-up view of lighter in Plate 256. (General Charles De Gaulle.)

Plate 261 • Chromium lighter with enamel military emblem made by Vulcan. Circa 1956. 2¼" H., 1½" W. $15.00 – 20.00.

Plate 262 • Brass and plastic butane pocket lighter made in Japan. Circa 1993. 2⅞" H., 1⅛" W. $5.00 – 10.00.

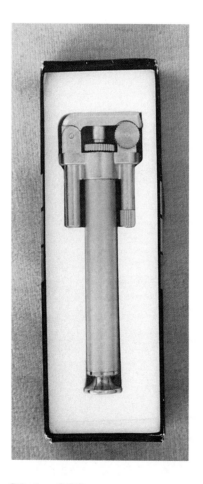

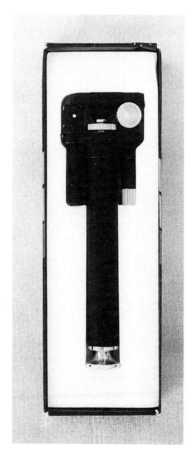

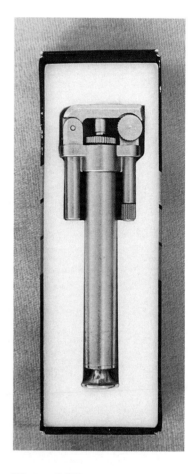

Plate 263 • "Happy Days" brass finish lift-arm pocket butane lighter made by Yoshinaga Prince Co., Ltd. Circa 1988. 3¼" H., 1" W. $5.00 – 10.00 each.

Plate 264 • Same as Plate 263 in matte black finish.

Plate 265 • Same as Plate 263 in chromium finish.

Plate 266 • The "Mini Cadet" chromium with embossed leaf pattern pocket lighter made by Ronson in England. Circa 1959. 1⅜" H., 1¾" W. $10.00 – 20.00.

Plate 267 • Chrommium pocket lighter with a watch made by Eclydo Co. (Note: watch has a small second hand.) Circa early 1950's. 2½" H., 1⅝" W. $75.00 – 100.00.

Plate 268 • Brass heart-shaped pocket lighter with gift box, cloth pouch, cleaning brush, and instructions made by Elgin American. Circa early 1950's. 2⅛" H., 2⅜" W. $25.00 – 40.00.

Plate 269 • Gold-plated musical pocket lighter made by Crown (plays "Smoke Gets In Your Eyes"). Circa late 1940's. 2⅝" H., 2" W. $50.00 – 75.00.

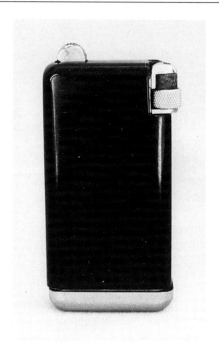

Plate 270 • The "Flaminare" chromium and enamel pocket lighter made by Parker Pen Co. Circa mid 1950's. 2¾" H., 1⅜" W. $20.00 – 40.00.

Plate 271 • Chromium butane pocket lighter made by Tanra Mfg. Co. Circa mid 1950's. 2¼" H., 1⅜" W. $10.00 – 20.00.

Plate 272 • Gold-plated replica butane lift-arm pocket lighter. Circa mid 1980's. 1⅞" H., ¾" W. $45.00 – 60.00.

Plate 273 • A unique brass lift-arm lever-action pocket lighter. Circa 1918. 1⅜" H., ⅞" W. $100.00 – 125.00.

Plate 274 • Back view of Plate 273.

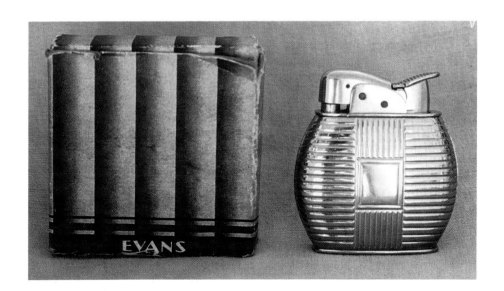

Plate 275 • Gold-plated pocket lighter with gift box made by Evans. Circa late 1930's. 2" H., 1⅞" W. $40.00 – 60.00.

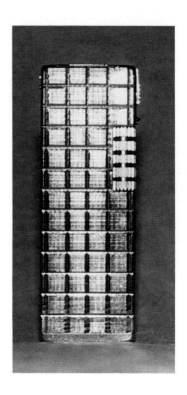

Plate 276 • The "Lucky" chromium pocket lighter with a unique lift arm and a built-in windscreen made by Thorens. Circa mid 1930's. 2" H., 1½" W. $80.00 – 110.00.

Plate 277 • Chromium butane replica lift-arm lighter made by Penguin. Circa late 1970's. 2⅝" H., ⅞" W. $10.00 – 20.00.

Plate 278 • Chromium pocket lighter with gift box made by A.T.C. Circa mid 1950's. 2¼" H., 1½" W. $10.00 – 20.00.

Plate 280 • The "Comet" chromium and plastic butane pocket lighter made by Ronson. Circa late 1950's. 2¼" H., 1½" W. $10.00 – 15.00.

Plate 279 • Silver-plated with leaf etched pattern made by Zippo. Circa 1994. 2¼" H., 1½" W. $45.00 – 60.00.

Plate 281 • Round chromium pocket lighter that has an English sixpence coin. Circa 1940. 1¾" H., 1½" W. $25.00 – 40.00.

Plate 282 • Gold-plated lift-arm pocket lighter with a wooden gift box. This is a replica of the 1928 model made by Colibri. Circa 1994. 1⅞" H., 1⅜" W. $60.00 – 90.00.

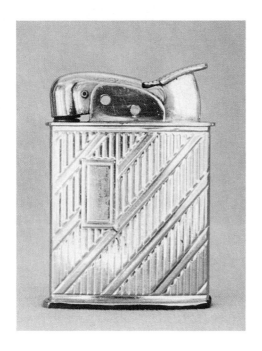

Plate 283 • Chromium pocket lighter made by Evans. Circa 1934. 2" H., 1½" W. $25.00 – 40.00.

Plate 284 • "Starfire" brass butane pocket lighter made by Ronson. Circa early 1960's. 2⅛" H., 1⅜" W. $10.00 – 15.00.

Plate 285 • Chromium lift-arm pocket lighter made by Polo in England. Circa 1932. 1¾" H., 1½" W. $50.00 – 75.00.

Plate 286 • Chromium pocket lighter made by Colibri. Circa mid 1950's. 1¾" H., 1⅝" W. $25.00 – 40.00.

Plate 287 • Gold-plated pocket lighter on a display stand made by Elgin American. Circa mid 1950's. 1¼" H., 2⅛" W. $40.00 – 60.00.

Plate 288 • Chromium lift-arm pocket lighter made by Polo in England. Circa 1932. 2⅛" H., 1⅝" W. $60.00 – 80.00.

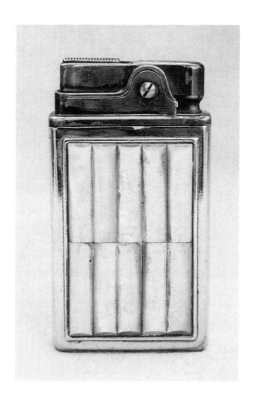

Plate 289 • Gold-plate with mother-of-pearl musical pocket lighter made by PAC. Circa early 1950's. 2⅝" H., 1⅜" W. $65.00 – 90.00.

Plate 290 • Back view of Plate 289 to show the keywind for the music box.

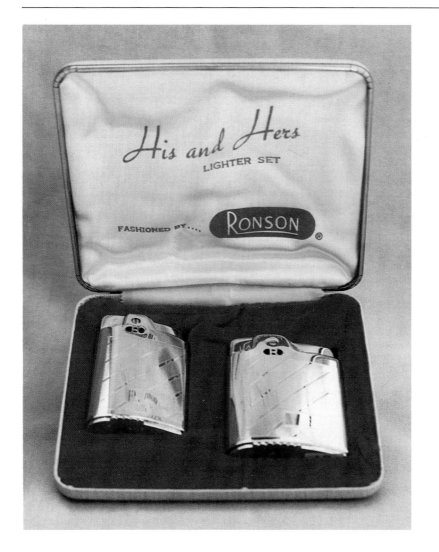

Plate 292 • Chromium butane pocket lighter made by Colibri. Circa mid 1970's. 2½" H., ⅞" W. $25.00 – 40.00.

Plate 291 • "His and Hers" chromium set of pocket lighters in a gift box made by Ronson. Circa 1955. Left lighter 2" H., 1⅜" W.; right lighter 2⅛" H., 2⅝" W. $50.00 – 70.00.

Plate 293 • Chromium lift-arm pocket lighter with a watch (Note: watch has a separate second hand) made by Malton. Circa late 1920's. 2" H., 1⅜" W. $175.00 – 225.00.

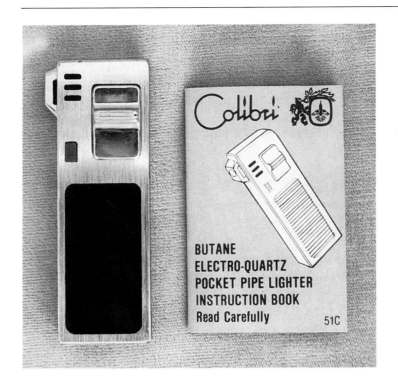

Plate 294 • Electro-Quartz chromium with leather accent butane pocket lighter made by Colibri. Circa 1960's. 3" H., 1" W. $30.00 – 60.00.

Plate 295 • Painted chromium pocket lighter commemorating Operation Desert Storm made in Korea. Circa early 1990's. 2¼" H., 1½" W. $10.00 – 15.00.

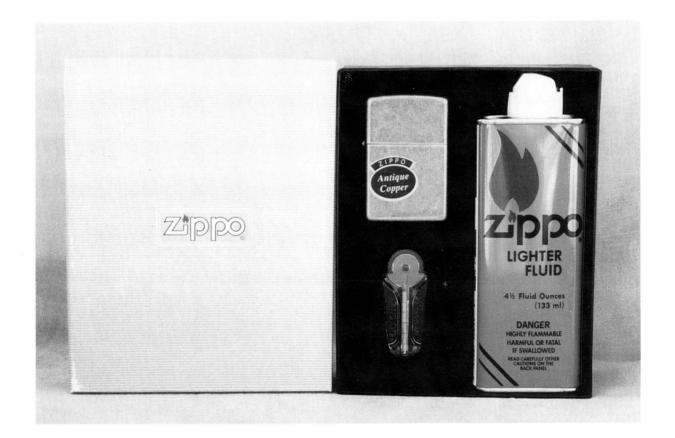

Plate 296 • Gift set including lighter with an antique copper finish, spare flints, and lighter fluid made by Zippo. Circa 1994. Lighter 2¼" H., 1½" W. $15.00 – 25.00.

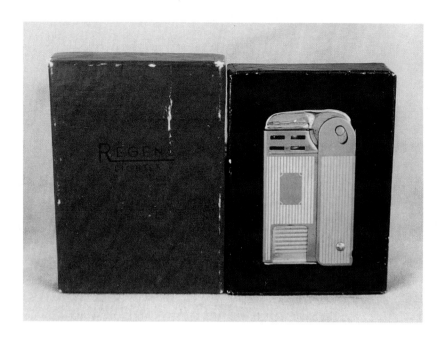

Plate 297 • Gold gilt etched pocket lighter in gift box with instructions made by Regens. Circa early 1950's. 2⅛" H., 1¼" W. $45.00 – 60.00.

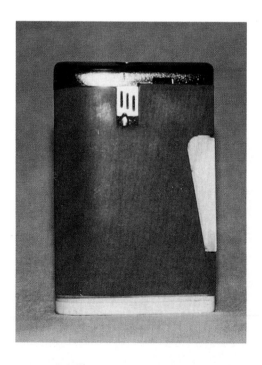

Plate 298 • The "Comet" chromium and plastic butane pocket lighter made by Ronson. (Similar Plate 280.) Circa late 1950's. 2¼" H., 1½" W. $10.00 – 15.00.

Plate 299 • O.T.L.S. Lighter Club's 10th anniversary lighter has a matte black finish made by Zippo. Circa 1994. 2¼" H., 1½" W. $10.00 – 20.00.

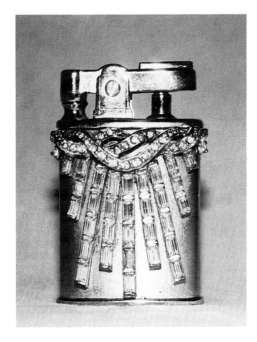

Plate 300 • The "Gem" chromium-finish lighter with rhinestones also has gift box and cloth bag. It is made by Ronson. Circa 1937. 2" H., 1¼" W. $60.00 – 85.00.

Plate 301 • Close-up view of Plate 300 to show detail of the rhinestones.

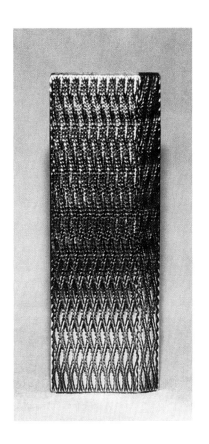

Plate 302 • The "Cadet" chromium pocket lighter made by Ronson in England. Circa 1959. 2⅛" H., 1¾" W. $20.00 – 35.00.

Plate 303 • Silver butane pocket lighter made by Cartier in France. Circa late 1970's. 2¾" H., 1" H. $80.00 – 100.00.

Plate 304 • Miniature chromium lift-arm pocket lighter made in Occupied Japan. Circa 1948. 1" H., ⅞" W. $20.00 – 40.00.

Plate 305 • Chromium butane pocket lighter made by Bentley. Circa mid 1950's. 1½" H., 2⅛" W. $10.00 – 20.00.

Plate 306 • Gold-plated and black enamel "Liter-pact" made by Ronson. (Compact in the center with a mirror.) Circa 1938. 2⅞" H., 2⅜" W. $100.00 – 150.00.

Plate 307 • Open view of Plates 306 and 308.

Plate 308 • Same as Plate 307 only in chromium and ivory enamel finish.

Plate 309 • Gold-plated lift-arm pocket lighter made by Dunhill in England. Circa 1934. 2½" H., ⅞" W. $175.00 – 225.00.

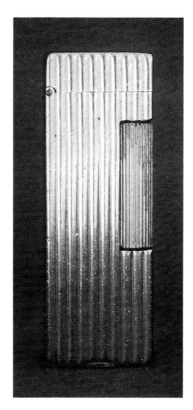

Plate 310 • Three-piece ceramic set made by Evans. Circa 1940's. Lighter 7" H., 3" Dia.; ashtray; 1⅜" H., 5½" W.; cigarette box 1¾" H., 4" W. $40.00 – 60.00.

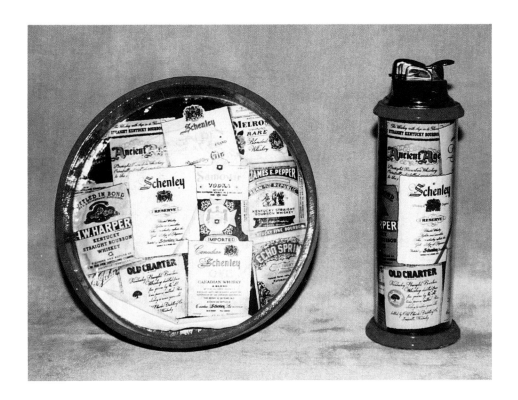

Plate 311 • Two-piece set made by Evans. Lighter 7" H., 2⅜" Dia. at base; ashtray 1½" H., 6½" Dia. $25.00 – 40.00.

Plate 312 • "Queen Anne" two-piece set made by Ronson. Circa 1936. Lighter 2⅝" H., 3⅛" W.; cigarette holder 2⅞" H., 2½" Dia. $20.00 – 30.00.

Plate 313 • Two-piece black marble and chromium "Nordic" set made by Ronson. Circa 1955. Lighter 3" H., 2¾" Dia.; cigarette holder 2⅞" H., 2¼" Dia. $20.00 – 40.00.

Plate 314 • Brass, white, and clear Lucite three-piece set made by Evans. (Each piece has a picture of a rainbow trout decorating it.) Circa early 1950's. Lighter 3½" H., 2⅝" W.; cigarette box 1¾" H., 4¼" W.; pen holder ¾" H., 3¼" W. $60.00 – 75.00.

Plate 315 • Brass-trimmed ceramic three-piece set made by Stylebuilt Accessories. Circa early 1950's. Lighter 3¾" H., 3⅛" W; ashtray 1¼" H., 3¾" Dia; cigarette holder 2¾" H., 3⅛" W. $25.00 – 40.00.

Plate 316 • Lighter is ceramic lamp and cat on a book (the pull chain operates the lighter). The tall center of the wooden box holds the cigarettes and the ashtray is recessed on the right side, also has a built in music box. Made by Venus. Circa late 1930's. 7¾" H., 11¾" W. $100.00 – 125.00.

Plate 317 • View of the open cigarette box. When open the cigarettes move up and down and the music box plays.

— TABLE LIGHTERS —

Plate 318 • Brass candlestick holder table lighter (lever on the right side above the finger hole handle operates the lighter at the top of the candle). Circa early 1920's. 5½" H., 3½" W. at base. $100.00 – 125.00.

Plate 319 • Chromium and blue marble-like plastic made in Japan (unique lighter mechanism). Circa early 1950's. 3½" H., 1½" Dia. at base. $20.00 – 30.00.

Plate 320 • P-51 Mustang chromium airplane table lighter made by Negbaur in Germany. (Lights by turning the propeller.) Circa 1948. 3" H., 6⅜" W., 6¼" wing span. $60.00 – 80.00.

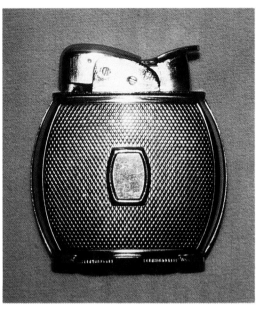

Plate 321 • Brass "Spirit of St. Louis" airplane with rubber tires made by SWANK. (Lights by turning the propeller.) Circa late 1940's. 1¾" H., 5⅜" W., 6⅝" wing span. $60.00 – 80.00.

Plate 322 • Small chromium table lighter made by Evans. Circa 1934. 2" H., 1⅞" W. $20.00 – 30.00.

Plate 323 • Chromium table lighter. (Lights when it is picked up.) Circa mid 1950's. 2⅜" H., 3" W. $20.00 – 30.00.

Plate 324 • Similar to plate 323 with a different textured finish.

Plate 325 • Silver-plate and glass table lighter made by Hy Glo. Circa late 1930's. 2½" H., 2¼" Dia. $35.00 – 50.00.

Plate 326 • Chromium ship's wheel table lighter made by Hamilton. (Lights by turning the wheel.) Circa late 1930's. 5⅛" H., 2¾" Dia. at base. $40.00 – 60.00.

Plate 327 • Metal and glass parlor lighter with wick snuffer in place. Circa 1860's. 4½" H., 1⅞" Dia. at base. $90.00 – 120.00.

Plate 328 • The "Saturn" chromium butane table lighter made by Ronson. Circa early 1960's. 4" H., 2" Dia. $15.00 – 20.00.

Plate 329 • Brass and ceramic table lighter made by Penguin. Circa late 1960's. 3¼" H., 1⅞" Dia. $10.00 – 20.00.

Plate 330 • Ceramic butane drum table lighter made by TIC in Hawaii. Circa early 1970's. 4¾" H., 2½" Dia. $10.00 – 20.00.

Plate 33l • Brass and green marble table lighter made by Evans. Circa mid 1930's. 3⅝" H., 3" Dia. at base. $30.00 – 45.00.

Plate 332 • Chromium and leather butane table lighter made by Querria in France. Circa late 1960's. 3¾" H., 2⅛" W. $40.00 – 50.00.

Plate 333 • Goldtone metal butane table lighter (lights by pushing the world button in the center) made by Monarch. Souvenir of the World's Fair in New York. Circa 1961. 2¼" H., 2¾" W. $40.00 – 60.00.

Plate 334 • Two-tone metal and plastic table lighter with a map of the world on the front and back made by B&B. Circa 1940's. 3⅛" H., 2⅞" W. $15.00 – 25.00.

Plate 335 • Chromium and leather table lighter made by D.R.P. in Germany. Circa early 1950's. 3¼" H., 4" W. $45.00 – 60.00.

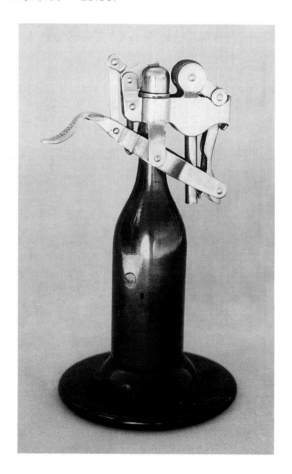

Plate 336 • Nickel-plate (on top) and brass table lighter made by Capitol. (Note: the complex lighter mechanism.) "Patented Sept. 17, 1912," circa 1913. 5" H., 2⅞" Dia at base. $125.00 – 200.00.

Plate 337 • Large chromium lift-arm table lighter made by A.T.M. Circa late 1940's. 4⅜" H., 3⅛" W. $40.00 – 60.00.

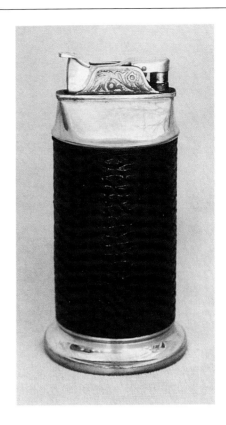

Plate 338 • Brass table lighter with a leather band made by Evans. Circa late 1920's. 3¾" H., 1⅞" Dia. at base. $40.00 – 60.00.

Plate 339 • The "Classic Jumbo" large chromium and leather lift-arm table lighter made in England by Brevete S.G.D.C. (Has a unique round knob to operate the flint wheel.) Circa 1930's. 4⅜" H., 3¼" W. $125.00 – 150.00.

Plate 340 • Chromium and wooden butane table lighter made in Japan. Circa 1970's. 4½" H., 1⅝" Dia. $10.00 – 15.00.

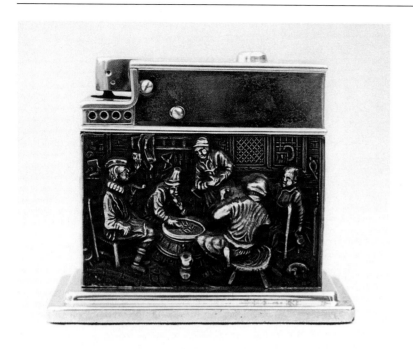

Plate 341 • Picturesque chromium table lighter made by Myflam. (Lights by pushing button on the top of the lighter.) Circa late 1940's. 2⅜" H., 3" W. $40.00 – 60.00.

Plate 342 • Brass and colored glass table lighter made by Strikalite. Circa late 1930's. 2¾" H., ¾" Dia. at base. $25.00 – 40.00.

Plate 343 • Chromium table lighter in the shape of a man's head made by W.B. Mfg. Co. Circa 1920's. (Lighter is where his tongue is, also has an ashtray in the back.) 2⅝" H., 4" W. $60.00 – 80.00.

Plate 344 • Brass and leather butane table lighter made in Italy. Circa mid 1970's. 4⅝" H., 2½" Dia. $20.00 – 30.00.

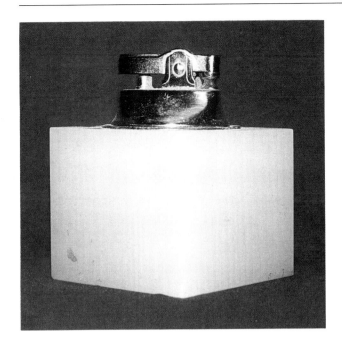

Plate 345 • Brass and marble cube table lighter. Circa mid 1950's. 3" H., 2¼" W. $20.00 – 40.00.

Plate 346 • Brass table lighter with a built-in Swiss-made Phinney-Walker alarm clock made by Evans. Circa late 1940's. 5" H., 2⅜" Dia. at base. $75.00 – 100.00.

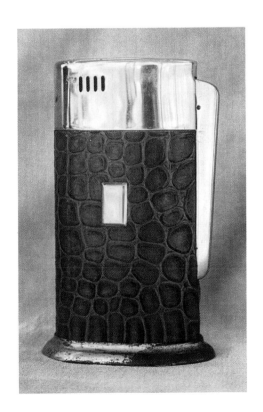

Plate 347 • Brass butane table lighter with a leather band made by Sparklet Devices Inc. Circa late 1950's. 4¼" H., 2⅝" W. $20.00 – 30.00.

Plate 348 • Large lift-arm pocket lighter made in Japan. Circa early 1950's. 7" H., 3½" W. $50.00 – 75.00.

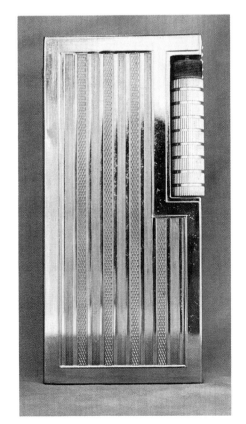

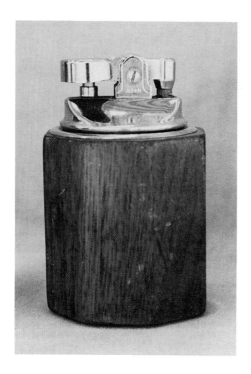

Plate 349 • Chromium and wooden butane table lighter made in Japan. Circa 1970's. 3" H., 2⅛" W. $10.00 – 15.00.

Plate 350 • Brass lighter with a clear Lucite base made by Evans. (Base has a golfer frozen in motion missing the ball.) Circa mid 1950's. 3¾" H., 2" W. $40.00 – 60.00.

Plate 351 • The "Flamidor" chromium automatic table lighter made by Brevete S.G.D.G. in France. Circa mid 1950's. 2⅞" H., 3⅜" W. $45.00 – 60.00.

Plate 352 • Red Devil's Flints display card. Circa 1993. 10¼" H., 6⅞" W. $.50 each.

Plate 353 • Brass and leather covered cigarette holder (to access cigarettes pull up on ring handle). Circa late 1940's. 5⅞" H., 3¼" Dia. at base. $10.00 – 20.00.

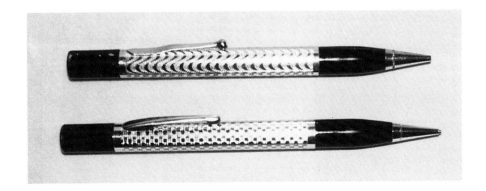

Plate 354 • Two chromium and enamel mechanical pencils, each with a different chromium finish (lighter under the cap). Circa mid 1950's. 5¼" H., ⅜" Dia. $15.00 – 20.00.

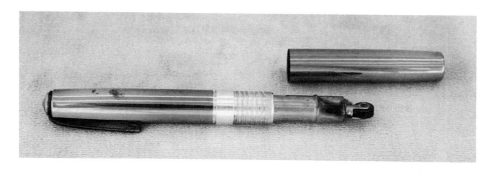

Plate 355 • Goldtone mechanical pencil with lighter under the cap made by All-bright in New York. Circa mid 1950's. 5" H., ½" Dia. $15.00 – 25.00.

Plate 356 • Chromium match box (with a sliding door to remove matches and striker on the bottom.) Circa late 1930's. 2" H., 1½" W. $10.00 – 20.00.

Plate 357 • Zippo tin that holds ten Zippo lighters for display. (Came empty so you could display the lighters of your choice.) Circa 1994. 2" H., 10" W. $10.00 – 15.00.

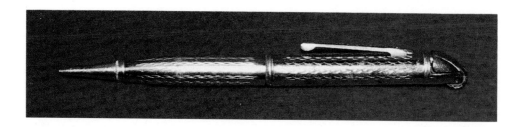

Plate 358 • Brass mechanical pencil with lighter at the top made by Stewart. Circa mid 1950's. 5⅛" H., ⅜" Dia. $10.00 – 20.00.

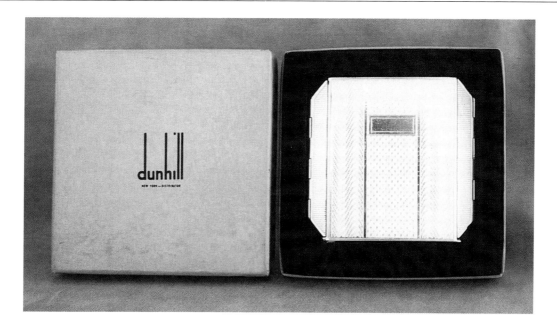

Plate 359 • Chromium cigarette package holder made by Dunhill. (Spring loaded to open for a pack of cigarettes.) Circa late 1950's. 3" H., 2¼" W. $40.00 – 60.00.

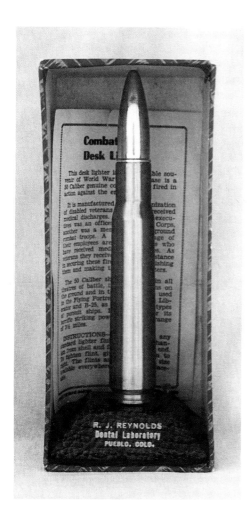

Plate 360 • Brass combat shell desk lighter (the 50 caliber shell is a memorable souvenir of W.W. II) with gift box and instructions, a product of Shaw-Barton. Circa late 1940's. 5½" H., ¾" Dia. $15.00 – 20.00.

Plate 361 • Brass and leatherette cigarette holder made by Amity. Circa late 1950's. 3⅝" H., 2⅜" W. $5.00 – 10.00.

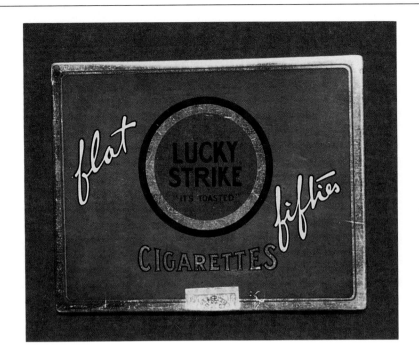

Plate 362 • Lucky Strike flat cigarette tin. Circa 1940's. 4⅜" H., 5¾" W. $20.00 – 30.00.

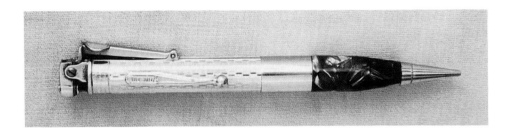

Plate 363 • The "Penciliter" in chromium and green-pearl plastic made by Ronson. Circa 1934. 5⅝" H., ½" Dia. $40.00 – 60.00.

Plate 364 • "Smokie the Smoking Pet" made by Adams. (Came with ten cigarettes and the dog could blow smoke rings.) Circa 1950's. Dog 1" H., 1½"; display 2¼" H., 3⅝" W. $25.00 – 40.00.

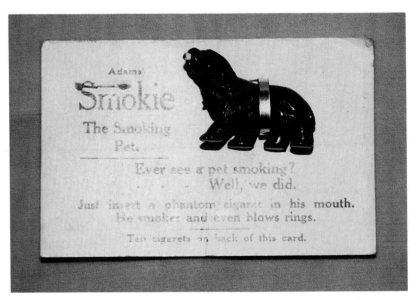

Plate 365 • Plastic roll-top cigarette dispenser with leather on the
sides made by Rolinx in England.
Circa 1952. 2⅜" H., 5¾" W.
$20.00 – 30.00.

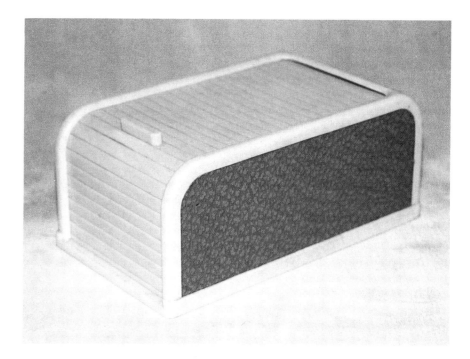

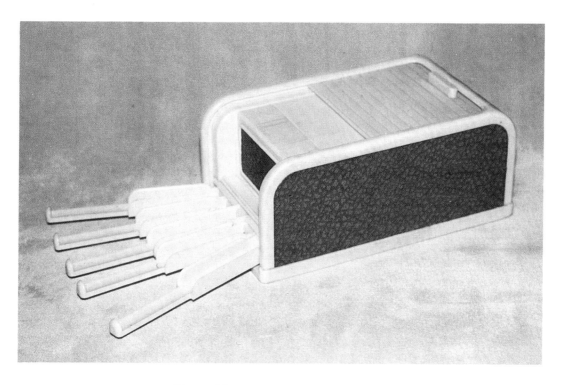

Plate 366 • Open view of Plate 365.

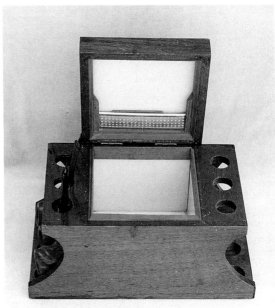

Plate 368 • Open view of Plate 367 to show glass lining.

Plate 367 • Wooden pipe rack and tobacco humidor, holds six pipes. Circa late 1940's. 5½" H., 10" W. $30.00 – 45.00.

Plate 369 • Brass cigarette caddy with a raised design in the center of the lid and a wooden handle made by Park Sherman. Circa 1940's. 1¼" H., 3½" W. $10.00 – 20.00.

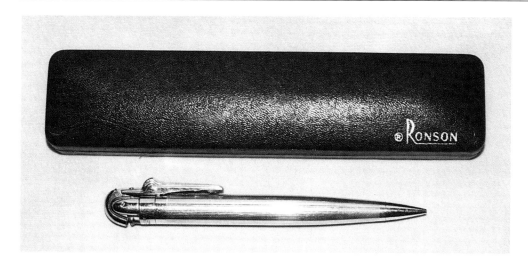

Plate 370 • 14K gold-plated "Penciliter" with gift box made by Ronson. Circa 1948. 5⅜" H., ½" Dia. $25.00 – 40.00.

Plate 371 • Chromium "Penciliter" made by Ronson. Circa 1948. 5⅜" H., ½" Dia. $25.00 – 40.00.

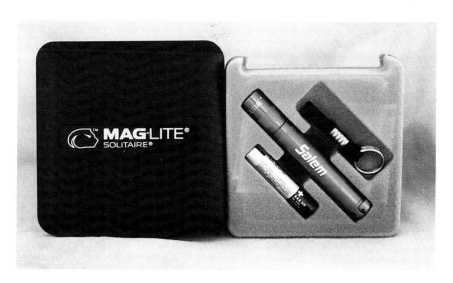

Plate 372 • Salem promotional Mag-Lite (flashlight, key ring, and battery) in a gift box made by Solitaire. Circa 1992. Flashlight 3⅛" H., ½" Dia. $10.00 – 15.00.

Plate 374 • Close-up view of Plate 373 to show detail.

Plate 373 • Meerschaum pipe (turns red after many years of smoking) made by Edward's pipe shop in Englewood, Colorado. Circa late 1960's. 3¼" H., 4¾" W. $50.00 – 75.00.

Plate 375 • Oriental wooden roll-top box (when top is rolled back the mechanism dispenses a cigarette) made in Japan. Circa 1930's. 2⅞" H., 4⅞" W. $50.00 – 75.00.

Plate 376 • Open view of Plate 375 showing the cigarette being dispensed by the wooden man's hands.

Plate 377 • Painted wooden bird cigarette dispenser made in Japan. Circa 1930's. 4½" H., 7½" W. $50.00 – 75.00.

Plate 378 • The bird in Plate 377 picks up a cigarette in its beak from the sliding compartment when the lever by its feet is moved downward.

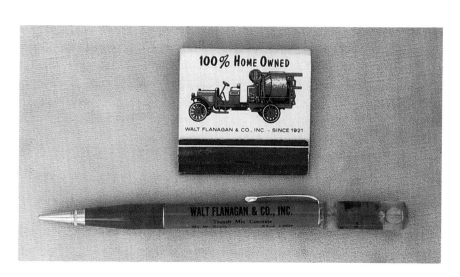

Plate 379 • Advertising match book and mechanical pencil (pencil has small truck that moves back and forth) for Walt Flanagan & Co., Denver, CO. Circa 1950s. Matches $3.00 – 5.00; pencil $20.00 – 30.00.

Plate 381 • Salem promotional gift (try to get the cigarettes in the pack). Circa 1950's. ½" H., 3⅞" Dia. $10.00 – 20.00.

Plate 380 • Brass pipe and match holder (matches are held inside the boot) made by Trophy Craft. Circa early 1940's 3⅞" H., 3¾" W. $20.00 – 40.00.

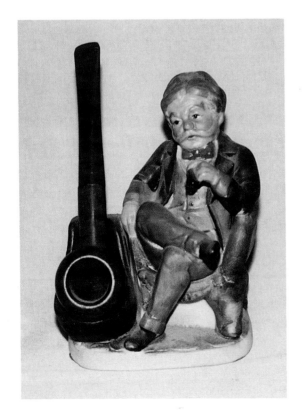

Plate 382 • Ceramic pipe holder. Circa 1960's. 4¾" H., 3⅝" W. $15.00 – 25.00.

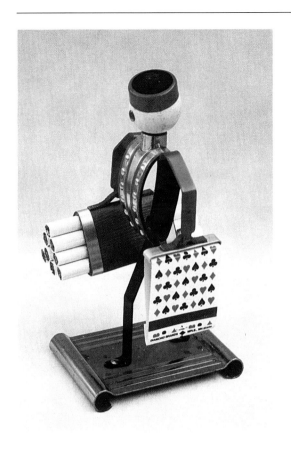

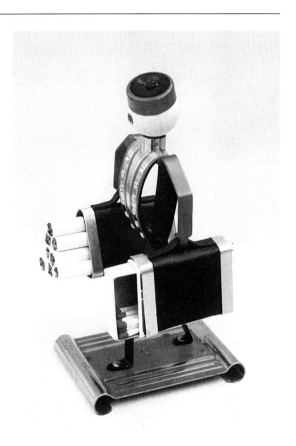

Plate 383 • Brass and enamel bellhop carrying cigarette and match book luggage made of brown leather and brass. 6" H., 3⅜" W. at base. $40.00 – 60.00

Plate 384 • Bellhop shown with black and brass luggage for cigarettes and match box.

Plate 385 • Bellhop shown with black and brass cigarette luggage and match book.

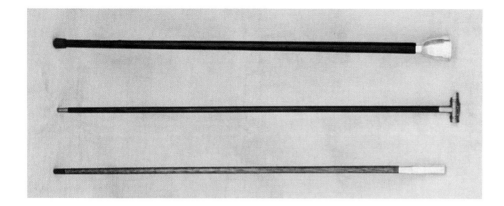

Plate 386 • Walking Canes. (a) 35¼" H., ⅞" Dia. (b) 36" H., ½" Dia. (c) 35" H., ⅝" Dia.

Plate 387 • Close-up of cane (a) in Plate 386 with its sterling silver handle and British coin (handle unscrews to reveal the lighter) from England. Circa 1920's. Handle 3" H., 2¼" Dia. $800.00 – 1500.00.

Plate 388 • Close-up view of cane (b) in Plate 386 showing its brass hinged match holder handle with striker on the lid. The other end has a "cat whistle" used for whistling at girls. Circa 1880's. Handle 1⅞" H., 2½" W. $600.00 – 900.00.

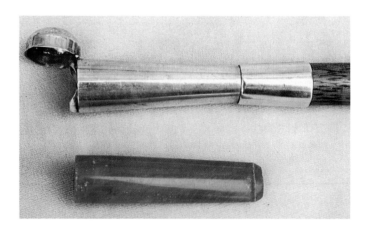

Plate 389 • Close-up view of (c) in Plate 386. Handle made of sterling silver, the top is hinged to reveal a cigar holder. Circa 1920's. Handle 4" H., ⅞" Dia.; cigar holder 2⅞" H., ¾" Dia. $650.00 – 900.00.

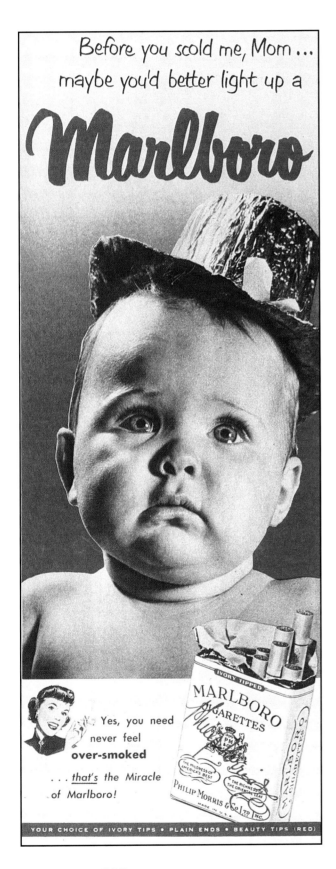

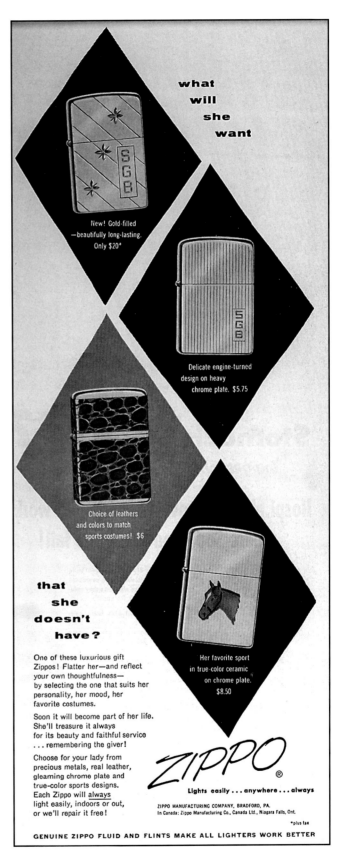

Plate 390 • *Colliers,* August 5, 1950.

Plate 391 • *Life,* November 8, 1954.

Plate 392 • *Esquire*, December 1949.

Plate 393 • *Esquire*, December 1949.

Plate 394 • *Harpers Bazaar*, October 1938.

Plate 395 • *Esquire*, January 1943.

Rogers

the finest in Smokers Accessories

SEE HOW IT CLOSES

This is a cross section of the Rogers Air-tite® Pouch, showing how *compound compression* on the lips of the "pouch within the pouch" holds in the freshness and aroma of the tobacco. Patented! If it isn't a Rogers, it isn't an Air-tite pouch!

Add to the enjoyment of smoking with a Rogers accessory. Ingeniously designed — strikingly styled! Great gifts for any smoker — especially yourself. Remember to ask for Rogers!

a. Rogers Air-tite® Tobacco Pouch—Combination Model—holds tobacco and pipe.
b. Peterson's DeLuxe Pipe, made in Ireland.
c. This Rogers Air-tite® Tobacco Pouch—the most popular tobacco pouch made.
d. RogerSpin® Ash Tray whisks away ashes and stubs. Positive closing action.
e. Rogers "24" Cigarette Case holds 24 REGULAR or 18 KING SIZE cigarettes.
f. Rogers "Coronet" Cigarette Case holds full pack. REGULAR and KING SIZE.
— each "Distinctively Rogers".
At finer shops **everywhere**:

Rogers imports, inc., NEW YORK 16, N.Y.

Plate 396 • *Esquire,* June 1955.

In this crystal filter,

HEALTH PROTECTION NO "FILTER CIGARETTE" CAN GIVE!

Even though you smoke a "filter tip" brand—take this common-sense step to *truly safer smoking:*

Filter every cigarette you smoke with a Denicotea Crystal Filter cigarette holder. *And see for yourself —in the Denicotea filter itself —the amazing extra protection you get!*

A fresh Denicotea filter, as shown above, is *crystal-clear in color.* Below are three test filters—each after smoking just 20 cigarettes of leading "filter tip" brands.

Brand A   Brand B   Brand C

Each has turned brown with absorbed tars and nicotine— irritants *passed* by the cigarette's "filter tip," but *trapped* by Denicotea's dramatically superior filtering action. *Proof* that no matter *which* brand of cigarettes you smoke *you'll* enjoy more smoking pleasure, greater peace of mind *with Denicotea!*

Makes *your* brand—*any* brand—safer to smoke!

Used and highly recommended by many physicians and dentists all over the world.
The smart, slim Denicotea Holder comes in various lengths, finishes and colors. **2.50** and **3.50** including extra filters. At stores everywhere.

dunhill
DE-NICOTEA
CRYSTAL FILTER
CIGARETTE HOLDER

Plate 397 • *Life,* September 20, 1954.

Plate 398 • *Esquire,* March 1943.

Plate 399 • *Life,* December 4, 1939.

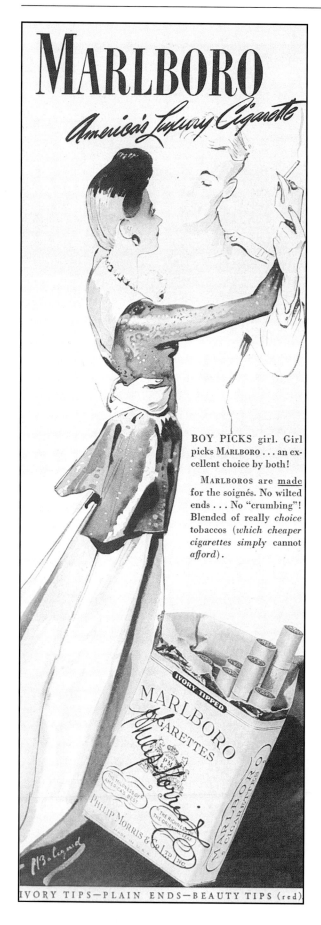

BOY PICKS girl. Girl picks MARLBORO ... an excellent choice by both!

MARLBOROS are made for the soignés. No wilted ends ... No "crumbing"! Blended of really *choice* tobaccos (*which cheaper cigarettes simply cannot afford*).

Plate 400 • *Esquire,* January 1943.

Plate 401 • *Esquire,* December 1949.

Just picture Dad, for example, in his favorite lounge chair, with his new Ash-Away smoker conveniently at his side. At a press of the button, stubs and ashes drop safely away ...no smoke, no smudge, no odors, no fire hazard. There are seven different Ash-Away styles in all, to fit every taste, every purse. All beautifully designed, sturdily made. At leading stores everywhere. Ash-Aways are made by Chicago Metallic Mfg. Co., Chicago 9.

Plate 402 • *Popular Mechanics*, December 1948.

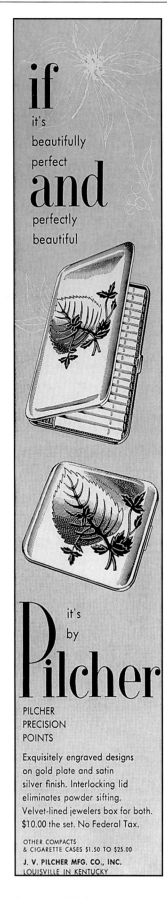

Plate 403 • *Esquire,*
December 1949.

Plate 404 • *Life,*
December 4, 1939.

Plate 405 • *Esquire,* December 1949.

Plate 406 • *Life*, December 4, 1954.

Plate 407 • *Esquire,* December 1949.

RONSON ADONIS. Slim as a
fine watch, $12.50. Other finishes for men
and women $10 to $200 (plus tax)

RONSON STANDARD.
Ever-popular for pocket or purse.
Trim and attractive, $6.00.

RONSON WHIRLWIND. Windproof
with disappearing windshield; genuine pigskin
$9. Others from $7.50.

RONSON QUEEN ANNE set.
Exquisite table lighter, cigarette urn and tray;
heavy silverplate $27.50 (plus tax)

RONSON CROWN Table Lighter;
popular favorite in heavy silverplate.
$11 (plus tax)

RONSON TEN-A-CASE. Cigarette case
with efficient built-in Ronson lighter.
$17.50. Other combinations from $10.

RONSON PENCILITER.
Lights...Writes! 14 K.
Gold Filled $15 (plus tax).
In precious Rhodium, plate
$10 (no Fed. Tax)

RONSON DIANA. Slim new
Table Lighter in heavy silverplate; monogram
shield. $8.50 (plus tax)

THERE'S A RONSON LIGHTER exactly right for every name on
your list! A Ronson to murmur "Love to my darling." Or to say
"You're a great guy!" to the boss. With any Ronson you choose, you're
giving a Merry Christmas—plus years of obedient lights. For every
Ronson is precision built to fine jewelry standards for long, dependable
service. Every Ronson features the famous, one-finger, one-motion safety
action—"press, it's lit!... release, it's out! *Safely out the instant
you lift your finger.*" See Ronson's big selection at your favorite store!

Tune in Ronson's "20 Questions" Saturday nights (Sunday nights, Pacific Coast),
Mutual Network... and Ronson's "Johnny Desmond Show" Sunday nights, Mutual
Network (Monday nights, Pacific Coast). See and hear Ronson on television, too!

RONSON Newark, N.J. Toronto, Ont. London, Eng.

everybody
is waiting
for a

RONSON
WORLD'S GREATEST LIGHTER

Plate 408 • *Esquire*, December 1949.

*You could give her
the world on a string,
but...*

she'd **rather have a Ronson**

From her favorite flame...a
Ronson pocket lighter is the perfect
gift, with or *without* strings attached.
As a birthday present, to celebrate
a special anniversary, or as a
wonderful spur-of-the-moment gift,
you simply can't miss with a Ronson.

There are so many pocket lighter
styles to choose from in Ronson's
smart assortment for women — in
gold and silver, in exciting colors,
in patterns and leathers. No matter
which you select, your gift of a
Ronson makes *you* the light of her
life, every single time she lights
a cigarette.

Shown: Ronson Adonis
in satin finish with engraved design
at $8.95. Other Ronson pocket
lighters from $4.95 to $200.

look for the name

RONSON *world's greatest gift!*

©1954 RONSON CORPORATION

Plate 409 • *Life,* September 20, 1954.

Plate 410 • *Esquire,* June 1955.

Sleek and elegant... Ronson's new table lighters

Each design in the Ronson "Award Series" is a signed original from the studio of one of the world's outstanding designers. Each is topped by the revolutionary "Golden Plume", adding its gleaming elegance to the lighter. And each will be issued only in a limited edition which will never be repeated.

Designs shown: by Harold Sitterle, in precious porcelain; executed in Europe by world-famous Rosenthal Porcelain, 32.50 and 27.50, others from 20.00

©1954 RONSON CORPORATION   Available at fine department stores, jewelry stores and gift shops.   Look for the name RONSON world's greatest lighter

Plate 411 • *Life,* November 8, 1954.

Plate 412 • *Esquire*, December 1949.

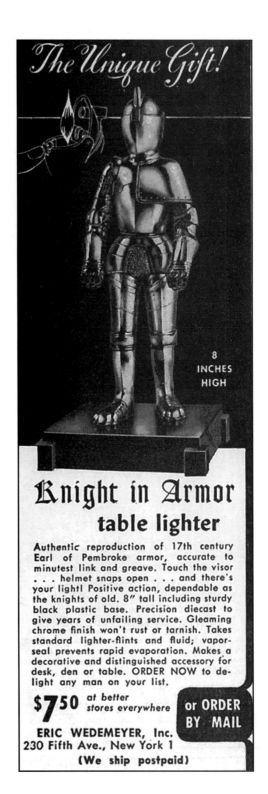

Plate 413 • *Esquire*, December 1949.

"SMART SET"
of the season
FOR EVERY TABLE AND DESK

Play SANTA with a NEW and DIFFER-
ENT cigarette lighter . . . the ASR
"Heritage." Handsome in simplicity
plus fine craftsmanship adds to smok-
ing pleasure. Finished in spark-
ling, non-tarnish
RHODIUM. (Also
available in
COPPER or
BRASS). (Guar-
ant'd by mfr.)
3 pc. set $25 PP.
LIGHTER ALONE (approx. 2¾x2¼) $12.50
(No C.O.D.'s, please)
KING NOVELTIES 69 Remsen Street
Brooklyn 2, N. Y.

Plate 414 • *Esquire,* December 1949.

GOOD FOR 1,000 LAUGHS

Everybody will want to use your **Bed Pan Ash Tray**,
with its riotous inscription. It really works—you
empty butts and ashes by pouring them right out of
the spout! Fine white glazed pottery, 6 inches long,
3 inches across. Order by mail—only $1.50, post-
paid. No C.O.D.'s, please. Write Dept. A-7.

THE SELDEN COOPER SHOP
Geo. Vanderbilt Hotel, Asheville, N. C.

Plate 415 • *Argosy,* July 1950.

Plate 416 • *Esquire,* January 1943.

RED CAP
always at your service

Full pack of
cigarettes in
one valise,
matches in the
other, remov-
able ashtray
base. He's 9¾
inches high, in
solid brass that
won't tarnish,
with a wooden
head and
bright red cap.
$4.95 tax free,
postage prepaid anywhere.
Send check or money order. Sorry, no COD's.
FREE—New 1950 catalog of gifts and gadgets.
DENNIS & CO., 17 East 48th St.
New York 17, N. Y.

Plate 417 • *Esquire,* December 1949.

lasts longer lights faster!

RONSONOL ®
LIGHTER FUEL

best
for
<u>all</u>
lighters

4 oz.
can
25¢

P.S. Use RONSON Redskin 'Flints'

by **RONSON** — world's greatest lighter specialists

Plate 418 • *Colliers,* August 12, 1950.

**New Realistic Pistol Lighter
Sure Fire Trigger Action**

Order Now
Only
$4⁹⁵

- Made Like Real Pistol
- Polished Silvery Finish
- Black Bone-like Handle
- 100% Satisfaction Guaranteed

For yourself or for a gift . . . A handsome automatic cigarette lighter Pistol replica (3" x 2½"). A sure eye catcher and it works every time. Order yours now! Send $4.95 and we prepay postage. C. O. D.'s—postage extra. Either way if not 100% satisfied, return within 5 days for full refund.

CENTRAL SALES CO.
Dept. 9, 5 No. Wabash Ave.
Chicago 2, Illinois

Please send......Pistol Lighters at $4.95 each.

NAME . . . .
ADDRESS . . . .
CITY. . . . . Zone. . . State . .
☐ Check ☐ Money Order ☐ C.O.D.

Plate 419 • *Argosy,* July 1950.

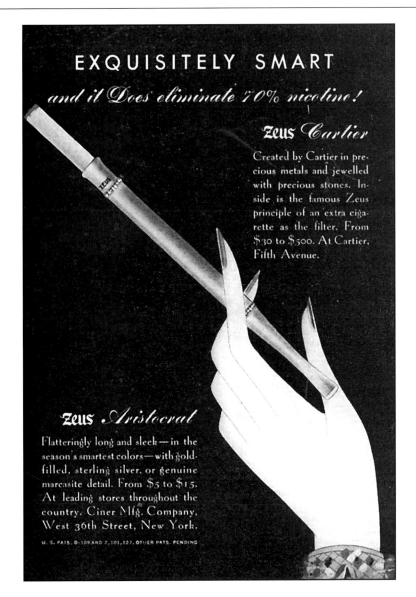

EXQUISITELY SMART
and it Does eliminate 70% nicotine!

Zeus *Cartier*

Created by Cartier in precious metals and jewelled with precious stones. Inside is the famous Zeus principle of an extra cigarette as the filter. From $30 to $500. At Cartier, Fifth Avenue.

Zeus *Aristocrat*

Flatteringly long and sleek — in the season's smartest colors — with gold-filled, sterling silver, or genuine marcasite detail. From $5 to $15. At leading stores throughout the country. Ciner Mfg. Company, West 36th Street, New York.

U. S. PATS. D-109 AND 2,101,127. OTHER PATS. PENDING

Plate 420 • *Harpers Bazaar*, October 1938.

Plate 421 • *Esquire*, December 1949.

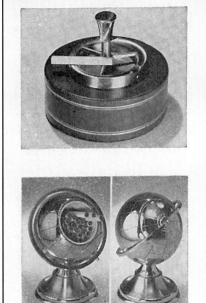

AUTOMATIC, SELF-CLEANING ash tray comes with a bronze top and wine, green, red or brown leather base with gold leaf tooling. Pressure on the plunger drops bottom disc and starts it whirling. Centrifugal force throws off ashes and cigarette stubs instantly. Keeps smoke and odors sealed in. Opens and cleans easily

SMOKE UP, relax, and contemplate the world. Give your den an international atmosphere with this global cigarette container. Gold-plated, it opens or shuts tightly with an easy movement of the meridian-like great circle. On a sturdy pedestal, the shiny world holds twenty cigarettes. When closed, it keeps them dust-free and fresh.

Plate 422 • *Esquire,* January 1943.

BOOKS ON COLLECTIBLES

This is only a partial listing of the books on antiques that are available from Collector Books. All books are well illustrated and contain current values. Most of the following books are available from your local bookseller, antique dealer, or public library. If you are unable to locate certain titles in your area, you may order by mail from COLLECTOR BOOKS, P.O. Box 3009, Paducah, KY 42002-3009. Customers with Visa or MasterCard may phone in orders from 7:00–4:00 CST, Monday–Friday, Toll Free 1-800-626-5420. Add $2.00 for postage for the first book ordered and $0.30 for each additional book. Include item number, title, and price when ordering. Allow 14 to 21 days for delivery.

DOLLS, FIGURES & TEDDY BEARS

2382	**Advertising Dolls**, Identification & Values, Robison & Sellers	$9.95
2079	**Barbie** Doll Fashions, Volume I, Eames	$24.95
3957	**Barbie** Exclusives, Rana	$18.95
3310	**Black Dolls**, 1820–1991, Perkins	$17.95
3873	**Black Dolls**, Book II, Perkins	$17.95
3810	**Chatty Cathy** Dolls, Lewis	$15.95
2021	Collector's **Male Action Figures**, Manos	$14.95
1529	Collector's Encyclopedia of **Barbie** Dolls, DeWein	$19.95
3727	Collector's Guide to **Ideal Dolls**, Izen	$18.95
3728	Collector's Guide to Miniature **Teddy Bears**, Powell	$17.95
4506	**Dolls in Uniform**, Bourgeois	$18.95
3967	Collector's Guide to **Trolls**, Peterson	$19.95
1067	**Madame Alexander** Dolls, Smith	$19.95
3971	**Madame Alexander** Dolls Price Guide #20, Smith	$9.95
2185	**Modern Collector's** Dolls I, Smith	$17.95
2186	**Modern Collector's** Dolls II, Smith	$17.95
2187	**Modern Collector's** Dolls III, Smith	$17.95
2188	**Modern Collector's** Dolls IV, Smith	$17.95
2189	**Modern Collector's** Dolls V, Smith	$17.95
3733	**Modern Collector's** Dolls, Sixth Series, Smith	$24.95
3991	**Modern Collector's** Dolls, Seventh Series, Smith	$24.95
3472	**Modern Collector's** Dolls Update, Smith	$9.95
3972	Patricia Smith's **Doll Values**, Antique to Modern, 11th Edition	$12.95
3826	Story of **Barbie**, Westenhouser	$19.95
1513	**Teddy Bears & Steiff** Animals, Mandel	$9.95
1817	**Teddy Bears & Steiff** Animals, 2nd Series, Mandel	$19.95
2084	**Teddy Bears, Annalee's & Steiff** Animals, 3rd Series, Mandel	$19.95
1808	Wonder of **Barbie**, Manos	$9.95
1430	World of **Barbie** Dolls, Manos	$9.95

TOYS, MARBLES & CHRISTMAS COLLECTIBLES

3427	**Advertising Character** Collectibles, Dotz	$17.95
2333	Antique & Collector's **Marbles**, 3rd Ed., Grist	$9.95
3827	Antique & Collector's **Toys**, 1870–1950, Longest	$24.95
3956	Baby Boomer **Games**, Identification & Value Guide, Polizzi	$24.95
1514	Character **Toys** & Collectibles, Longest	$19.95
1750	Character **Toys** & Collector's, 2nd Series, Longest	$19.95
3717	**Christmas** Collectibles, 2nd Edition, Whitmyer	$24.95
1752	**Christmas** Ornaments, Lights & Decorations, Johnson	$19.95
3874	Collectible Coca-Cola Toy **Trucks**, deCourtivron	$24.95
2338	Collector's Encyclopedia of **Disneyana**, Longest, Stern	$24.95
2151	Collector's Guide to **Tootsietoys**, Richter	$16.95
3436	Grist's Big Book of **Marbles**	$19.95
3970	Grist's Machine-Made & Contemporary **Marbles**, 2nd Ed.	$9.95
3732	**Matchbox®** Toys, 1948 to 1993, Johnson	$18.95
3823	**Mego** Toys, An Illustrated Value Guide, Chrouch	15.95
1540	**Modern Toys** 1930–1980, Baker	$19.95
3888	**Motorcycle** Toys, Antique & Contemporary, Gentry/Downs	$18.95
3891	Schroeder's Collectible **Toys**, Antique to Modern Price Guide	$17.95
1886	Stern's Guide to **Disney** Collectibles	$14.95
2139	Stern's Guide to **Disney** Collectibles, 2nd Series	$14.95
3975	Stern's Guide to **Disney** Collectibles, 3rd Series	$18.95
2028	**Toys**, Antique & Collectible, Longest	$14.95
3975	**Zany Characters** of the Ad World, Lamphier	$16.95

JEWELRY, HATPINS, WATCHES & PURSES

1712	Antique & Collector's **Thimbles** & Accessories, Mathis	$19.95
1748	Antique **Purses**, Revised Second Ed., Holiner	$19.95
1278	Art Nouveau & Art Deco **Jewelry**, Baker	$9.95
3875	Collecting Antique **Stickpins**, Kerins	$16.95
3722	Collector's Ency. of **Compacts, Carryalls & Face Powder Boxes**, Mueller	$24.95
3992	Complete Price Guide to **Watches**, #15, Shugart	$21.95
1716	Fifty Years of Collector's **Fashion Jewelry**, 1925-1975, Baker	$19.95
1424	**Hatpins** & Hatpin Holders, Baker	$9.95
1181	100 Years of Collectible **Jewelry**, Baker	$9.95
2348	20th Century Fashionable Plastic **Jewelry**, Baker	$19.95
3830	Vintage **Vanity Bags & Purses**, Gerson	$24.95

FURNITURE

1457	American **Oak** Furniture, McNerney	$9.95
3716	American **Oak** Furniture, Book II, McNerney	$12.95
1118	Antique **Oak** Furniture, Hill	$7.95
2132	Collector's Encyclopedia of **American** Furniture, Vol. I, Swedberg	$24.95
2271	Collector's Encyclopedia of **American** Furniture, Vol. II, Swedberg	$24.95
3720	Collector's Encyclopedia of **American** Furniture, Vol. III, Swedberg	$24.95
1437	Collector's Guide to **Country** Furniture, Raycraft	$9.95
3878	Collector's Guide to **Oak** Furniture, George	$12.95
1755	Furniture of the **Depression Era**, Swedberg	$19.95
3906	**Heywood-Wakefield** Modern Furniture, Rouland	$18.95
1965	**Pine** Furniture, Our American Heritage, McNerney	$14.95
1885	**Victorian** Furniture, Our American Heritage, McNerney	$9.95
3829	**Victorian** Furniture, Our American Heritage, Book II, McNerney	$9.95
3869	**Victorian** Furniture books, 2 volume set, McNerney	$19.90

INDIANS, GUNS, KNIVES, TOOLS, PRIMITIVES

1868	Antique **Tools**, Our American Heritage, McNerney	$9.95
2015	Archaic **Indian** Points & Knives, Edler	$14.95
1426	**Arrowheads** & Projectile Points, Hothem	$7.95
1668	**Flint Blades** & Projectile Points of the North American Indian, Tully	$24.95
2279	**Indian** Artifacts of the Midwest, Hothem	$14.95
3885	**Indian** Artifacts of the Midwest, Book II, Hothem	$16.95
1964	**Indian** Axes & Related Stone Artifacts, Hothem	$14.95
2023	**Keen Kutter** Collectibles, Heuring	$14.95
3887	Modern **Guns**, Identification & Values, 10th Ed., Quertermous	$12.95
2164	**Primitives**, Our American Heritage, McNerney	$9.95
1759	**Primitives**, Our American Heritage, Series II, McNerney	$14.95
3325	Standard **Knife** Collector's Guide, 2nd Ed., Ritchie & Stewart	$12.95

PAPER COLLECTIBLES & BOOKS

1441	Collector's Guide to **Post Cards**, Wood	$9.95
2081	Guide to Collecting **Cookbooks**, Allen	$14.95
3969	Huxford's **Old Book** Value Guide, 7th Ed.	$19.95
3821	Huxford's **Paperback** Value Guide	$19.95
2080	Price Guide to **Cookbooks & Recipe Leaflets**, Dickinson	$9.95
2346	**Sheet Music** Reference & Price Guide, Pafik & Guiheen	$18.95

OTHER COLLECTIBLES

2280	Advertising **Playing Cards**, Grist	$16.95
2269	Antique **Brass & Copper** Collectibles, Gaston	$16.95
1880	Antique **Iron**, McNerney	$9.95
3872	Antique **Tins**, Dodge	$24.95
1714	**Black** Collectibles, Gibbs	$19.95
1128	**Bottle** Pricing Guide, 3rd Ed., Cleveland	$7.95
3959	**Cereal Box** Bonanza, The 1950's, Bruce	$19.95
3718	Collector's **Aluminum**, Grist	$16.95
3445	Collectible **Cats**, An Identification & Value Guide, Fyke	$18.95
1634	Collector's Ency. of Figural & Novelty **Salt & Pepper Shakers**, Davern	$19.95
2020	Collector's Ency. of Figural & Novelty **Salt & Pepper Shakers**, Vol. II, Davern	$19.95
2018	Collector's Encyclopedia of **Granite Ware**, Greguire	$24.95
3430	Collector's Encyclopedia of **Granite Ware**, Book II, Greguire	$24.95
3879	Collector's Guide to Antique **Radios**, 3rd Ed., Bunis	$18.95
1916	Collector's Guide to **Art Deco**, Gaston	$14.95
3880	Collector's Guide to **Cigarette Lighters**, Flanagan	$17.95
1537	Collector's Guide to **Country Baskets**, Raycraft	$9.95
3966	Collector's Guide to **Inkwells**, Identification & Values, Badders	$18.95
3881	Collector's Guide to **Novelty Radios**, Bunis/Breed	$18.95
3729	Collector's Guide to **Snow Domes**, Guarnaccia	$18.95
3730	Collector's Guide to **Transistor Radios**, Bunis	$15.95
2276	**Decoys**, Kangas	$24.95
1629	**Doorstops**, Identification & Values, Bertoia	$9.95
3968	**Fishing Lure** Collectibles, Murphy/Edmisten	$24.95
3817	**Flea Market Trader**, 9th Ed., Huxford	$12.95
3819	**General Store Collectibles**, Wilson	$24.95
2215	Goldstein's **Coca-Cola** Collectibles	$16.95
3884	Huxford's **Collector's Advertising**, 2nd Ed.	$24.95
2216	**Kitchen Antiques**, 1790–1940, McNerney	$14.95
1782	1,000 **Fruit Jars**, 5th Edition, Schroeder	$5.95
3321	Ornamental & Figural **Nutcrackers**, Rittenhouse	$16.95
2026	**Railroad** Collectibles, 4th Ed., Baker	$14.95
1632	**Salt & Pepper Shakers**, Guarnaccia	$9.95
1888	**Salt & Pepper Shakers** II, Identification & Value Guide, Book II, Guarnaccia	$14.95
2220	**Salt & Pepper Shakers** III, Guarnaccia	$14.95
3443	**Salt & Pepper Shakers** IV, Guarnaccia	$18.95
2096	**Silverplated Flatware**, Revised 4th Edition, Hagan	$14.95
1922	Standard **Old Bottle** Price Guide, Sellari	$14.95
3892	**Toy & Miniature Sewing Machines**, Thomas	$18.95
3828	Value Guide to **Advertising Memorabilia**, Summers	$18.95
3977	Value Guide to **Gas Station** Memorabilia	$24.95
3444	**Wanted to Buy**, 5th Edition	$9.95

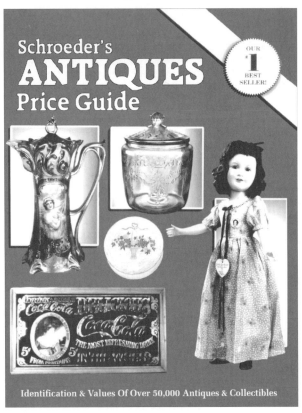